PLAY ON SHAKESPEARE

Henry IV
Part 2

PLAY ON SHAKESPEARE

All's Well That Ends Well	Virginia Grise
Antony and Cleopatra	Christopher Chen
As You Like It	David Ivers
The Comedy of Errors	Christina Anderson
Coriolanus	Sean San José
Cymbeline	Andrea Thome
Edward III	Octavio Solis
Hamlet	Lisa Peterson
Henry IV	Yvette Nolan
Henry V	Lloyd Suh
Henry VI	Douglas P. Langworthy
Henry VIII	Caridad Svich
Julius Caesar	Shishir Kurup
King John	Brighde Mullins
King Lear	Marcus Gardley
Love's Labour's Lost	Josh Wilder
Macbeth	Migdalia Cruz
Measure for Measure	Aditi Brennan Kapil
The Merchant of Venice	Elise Thoron
The Merry Wives of Windsor	Dipika Guha
A Midsummer Night's Dream	Jeffrey Whitty
Much Ado About Nothing	Ranjit Bolt
Othello	Mfoniso Udofia
Pericles	Ellen McLaughlin
Richard II	Naomi Iizuka
Richard III	Migdalia Cruz
Romeo and Juliet	Hansol Jung
The Taming of the Shrew	Amy Freed
The Tempest	Kenneth Cavander
Timon of Athens	Kenneth Cavander
Titus Andronicus	Amy Freed
Troilus and Cressida	Lillian Groag
Twelfth Night	Alison Carey
The Two Gentlemen of Verona	Amelia Roper
The Two Noble Kinsmen	Tim Slover
The Winter's Tale	Tracy Young

Henry IV
Part 2

by
William Shakespeare

Modern verse translation by
Yvette Nolan

Dramaturgy by
Waylon Lenk

Arizona Center
for Medieval and
Renaissance Studies
ACMRS PRESS
Arizona State University
Tempe, Arizona
2022

———

Publication of Play On Shakespeare is assisted by
generous support from the Hitz Foundation.
For more information, please visit www.playonshakespeare.org

———

Published by ACMRS Press
Arizona Center for Medieval and Renaissance Studies,
Arizona State University, Tempe, Arizona
www.acmrspress.com

Library of Congress Cataloging-in-Publication Data (for Volume 1)
Names: Nolan, Yvette, author. | Lenk, Waylon, contributor. | Shakespeare,
    William, 1564-1616. King Henry IV. Part 1.
Title: Henry IV. Part 1 / by William Shakespeare ; modern verse
    translation by Yvette Nolan ; dramaturgy by Waylon Lenk.
Description: Tempe, Arizona : ACMRS Press, 2022. | Series: Play on
    Shakespeare | Summary: "Featuring some of Shakespeare's most
    recognizable characters Henry IV, Part 1 delves into complicated
    questions of loyalty and kingship on and off the battlefield.
    Modernizing the language of the play, Yvette Nolan's translation
    carefully works at the seeds sown by Shakespeare-bringing to new
    life the characters and dramatic arcs of the original"-- Provided by
    publisher.
Identifiers: LCCN 2022006529 (print) | LCCN 2022006530 (ebook) |
    ISBN 9780866986847 (paperback) | ISBN 9780866986854 (ebook)
Subjects: LCSH: Henry IV, King of England, 1367-1413--Drama. | Great
    Britain--Kings and rulers--Drama. | LCGFT: Historical drama.
Classification: LCC PR2878.K2 N65 2022 (print) | LCC PR2878.K2
    (ebook) | DDC 822.3/3--dc23/eng/20220209
LC record available at https://lccn.loc.gov/2022006529
LC ebook record available at https://lccn.loc.gov/2022006530

Printed in the United States of America

We wish to acknowledge our gratitude
for the extraordinary generosity of the
Hitz Foundation

～

Special thanks to the Play on Shakespeare staff
Lue Douthit, CEO and Creative Director
Kamilah Long, Executive Director
Taylor Bailey, Associate Creative Director and Senior Producer
Summer Martin, Director of Operations
Amrita Ramanan as Senior Cultural Strategist and Dramaturg
Katie Kennedy, Publications Project Manager

～

Originally commissioned by the
Oregon Shakespeare Festival
Bill Rauch, Artistic Director
Cynthia Rider, Executive Director

In 2015, the Oregon Shakespeare Festival announced a new commissioning program. It was called "Play on!: 36 playwrights translate Shakespeare." It elicited a flurry of reactions. For some people this went too far: "You can't touch the language!" For others, it didn't go far enough: "Why not new adaptations?" I figured we would be on the right path if we hit the sweet spot in the middle.

Some of the reaction was due not only to the scale of the project, but its suddenness: 36 playwrights, along with 38 dramaturgs, had been commissioned and assigned to translate 39 plays, and they were already hard at work on the assignment. It also came fully funded by the Hitz Foundation with the shocking sticker price of $3.7 million.

I think most of the negative reaction, however, had to do with the use of the word "translate." It's been difficult to define precisely. It turns out that there is no word for the kind of subtle and rigorous examination of language that we are asking for. We don't mean "word for word," which is what most people think of when they hear the word translate. We don't mean "paraphrase," either.

The project didn't begin with 39 commissions. Linguist John McWhorter's musings about translating Shakespeare is what sparked this project. First published in his 1998 book *Word on the Street* and reprinted in 2010 in *American Theatre* magazine, he notes that the "irony today is that the Russians, the French, and other people in foreign countries possess Shakespeare to a much greater extent than we do, for the simple reason that they get to enjoy Shakespeare in the language they speak."

This intrigued Dave Hitz, a long-time patron of the Oregon Shakespeare Festival, and he offered to support a project that looked at Shakespeare's plays through the lens of the English we speak today. How much has the English language changed since Shakespeare? Is it possible that there are conventions in the early modern English of Shakespeare that don't translate to us today, especially in the moment of hearing it spoken out loud as one does in the theater?

How might we "carry forward" the successful communication between actor and audience that took place 400 years ago? "Carry forward," by the way, is what we mean by "translate." It is the fourth definition of *translate* in the Oxford English Dictionary.

As director of literary development and dramaturgy at the Oregon Shakespeare Festival, I was given the daunting task of figuring out how to administer the project. I began with Kenneth Cavander, who translates ancient Greek tragedies into English. I figured that someone who does that kind of work would lend an air of seriousness to the project. I asked him how might he go about translating from the source language of early modern English into the target language of contemporary modern English?

He looked at different kinds of speech: rhetorical and poetical, soliloquies and crowd scenes, and the puns in comedies. What emerged from his tinkering became a template for the translation commission. These weren't rules exactly, but instructions that every writer was given.

First, do no harm. There is plenty of the language that doesn't need translating. And there is some that does. Every playwright had different criteria for assessing what to change.

Second, go line-by-line. No editing, no cutting, no "fixing." I want the whole play translated. We often cut the gnarly bits in

Shakespeare for performance. What might we make of those bits if we understood them in the moment of hearing them? Might we be less compelled to cut?

Third, all other variables stay the same: the time period, the story, the characters, their motivations, and their thoughts. We designed the experiment to examine the language.

Fourth, and most important, the language must follow the same kind of rigor and pressure as the original, which means honoring the meter, rhyme, rhetoric, image, metaphor, character, action, and theme. Shakespeare's astonishingly compressed language must be respected. Trickiest of all: making sure to work within the structure of the iambic pentameter.

We also didn't know which of Shakespeare's plays might benefit from this kind of investigation: the early comedies, the late tragedies, the highly poetic plays. So we asked three translators who translate plays from other languages into English to examine a Shakespeare play from each genre outlined in the *First Folio*: Kenneth took on *Timon of Athens,* a tragedy; Douglas Langworthy worked on the *Henry the Sixth* history plays, and Ranjit Bolt tried his hand at the comedy *Much Ado about Nothing.*

Kenneth's *Timon* received a production at the Alabama Shakespeare in 2014 and it was on the plane ride home that I thought about expanding the project to include 39 plays. And I wanted to do them all at once. The idea was to capture a snapshot of contemporary modern English. I couldn't oversee that many commissions, and when Ken Hitz (Dave's brother and president of the Hitz Foundation) suggested that we add a dramaturg to each play, the plan suddenly unfolded in front of me. The next day, I made a simple, but extensive, proposal to Dave on how to commission and develop 39 translations in three years. He responded immediately with "Yes."

My initial thought was to only commission translators who translate plays. But I realized that "carry forward" has other meanings. There was a playwright in the middle of the conversation 400 years ago. What would it mean to carry *that* forward?

For one thing, it would mean that we wanted to examine the texts through the lens of performance. I am interested in learning how a dramatist makes sense of the play. Basically, we asked the writers to create performable companion pieces.

I wanted to tease out what we mean by contemporary modern English, and so we created a matrix of writers who embodied many different lived experiences: age, ethnicity, gender-identity, experience with translations, geography, English as a second language, knowledge of Shakespeare, etc.

What the playwrights had in common was a deep love of language and a curiosity about the assignment. Not everyone was on board with the idea and I was eager to see how the experiment would be for them. They also pledged to finish the commission within three years.

To celebrate the completion of the translations, we produced a festival in June 2019 in partnership with The Classic Stage Company in New York to hear all 39 of them. Four hundred years ago I think we went to *hear* a play; today we often go to *see* a play. In the staged reading format of the Festival, we heard these plays as if for the first time. The blend of Shakespeare with another writer was seamless and jarring at the same time. Countless actors and audience members told us that the plays were understandable in ways they had never been before.

Now it's time to share the work. We were thrilled when Ayanna Thompson and her colleagues at the Arizona Center for Medieval and Renaissance Studies offered to publish the translations for us.

I ask that you think of these as marking a moment in time.

The editions published in this series are based on the scripts that were used in the Play on! Festival in 2019. For the purpose of the readings, there were cuts allowed and these scripts represent those reading drafts.

The original commission tasked the playwrights and dramaturg to translate the whole play. The requirement of the commission was for two drafts which is enough to put the ball in play. The real fun with these texts is when there are actors, a director, a dramaturg, and the playwright wrestling with them together in a rehearsal room.

The success of a project of this scale depends on the collaboration and contributions of many people. The playwrights and dramaturgs took the assignment seriously and earnestly and were humble and gracious throughout the development of the translations. Sally Cade Holmes and Holmes Productions, our producer since the beginning, provided a steady and calm influence.

We have worked with more than 1,200 artists in the development of these works. We have partnered with more than three dozen theaters and schools. Numerous readings and more than a dozen productions of these translations have been heard and seen in the United States as well as Canada, England, and the Czech Republic.

There is a saying in the theater that 80% of the director's job is taken care of when the production is cast well. Such was my luck when I hired Taylor Bailey, who has overseen every reading and workshop, and was the producer of the Festival in New York. Katie Kennedy has gathered all the essays, and we have been supported by the rest of the Play on Shakespeare team: Kamilah Long, Summer Martin, and Amrita Ramanan.

All of this has come to be because Bill Rauch, then artistic director of the Oregon Shakespeare Festival, said yes when Dave

Hitz pitched the idea to him in 2011. Actually he said, "Hmm, interesting," which I translated to "yes." I am dearly indebted to that 'yes.'

My gratitude to Dave, Ken, and the Hitz Foundation can never be fully expressed. Their generosity, patience, and unwavering belief in what we are doing has given us the confidence to follow the advice of Samuel Beckett: "Ever tried. Ever failed. No matter. Try again. Fail again. Fail better."

Play on!

Dr. Lue Douthit
CEO/Creative Director at Play on Shakespeare
October 2020

WHAT WAS I THINKING?

Henry IV, Part 2

by Yvette Nolan

I came to *Henry IV, Part 2* late, and also just in time. I had spent
the past two years immersed in *Henry IV, Part 1*, which had been
my initial assignment, and we had recently completed a 29-hour
workshop of my third draft in New York, when Lue approached
me — and dramaturg Waylon Lenk — about taking on the second
half of Prince Hal's journey to the crown.

The timeline was short. The playwright who was originally
slated to do the translation had received another big and important commission, and juggling the two was proving challenging. In
order to ensure that there was a full slate of translations for the
fast-approaching Play On! Festival in New York in June 2019, Lue
asked Waylon and I if we were game to tackle *Part 2*.

Okay, it wasn't *that* short. Lue asked us on May 27, 2018, and
the first day of the festival was May 29, 2019, so really, we had a
year, but compared to the luxurious pace of *Henry IV, Part 1*, taking
into consideration the other things that Waylon and I already had
in our calendars, this would need to be a much swifter process.
Nonetheless, we set a schedule, and four months later, on September 30th, we had a complete first draft.

The advantages I had entering into *Part 2* were many. The
rhythm of the language was still in my blood, beating like my heart
— bah-dum bah-dum bah-dum bah-dum bah-dum. Waylon and
I now had a shared language and an established process. I knew
many of these characters, Hal and the King, Falstaff and his crew,

Northumberland and Lady Percy. I had heard actors — those magical creatures — speak the words of *Part 1* trippingly on the tongue, and I wanted to deliver them text they deserved in *Part 2*.

My comfort with this second translation is evident in my notes from the time. Where I had been tentative and apprehensive at the beginning of *Part 1*, I was now enjoying the process. My emails to Waylon often contain the word "fun." I apologize for being a day late with a draft, explaining "I am having too much fun." A month later, another act is delivered with:

> *it's way easier and way more fun this go round*
> *though I still am stymied by things like "a singing-man of Windsor"*
> *and why that is insulting*

Three days after I delivered the last act of the first draft, Waylon sent me notes and a proposed new schedule. As we launched into the second draft, I told Waylon

> the language seems so much easier to me now, so I wonder if I have clarified enough, or just grown accustomed to the Shakespeare

Was the project turning me into a purist, one of those who were enraged by the idea of translations, insisting that people should just learn the original? And yet my understanding of the plays and the characters had deepened through the action of the translation. And I certainly had heavily translated some of the gnarlier bits. The jokes and lists, the arcane references and insults can be particularly challenging to the audience's comprehension, leaving the viewer behind when they stop to decipher the meaning of "virtue is of so little regard in these costermonger times that true valour is turned bear-herd."

WHAT WAS I THINKING?

In April, 2019, *Henry IV, Part 2* received a four-day workshop in New York; the experience was, once again, a gift.

The reason I had chosen *Henry IV, Part 1* in the first place was because I thought it the lighter, more hopeful of the two parts. I knew *Part 2* was darker; the New York workshop showed me just how much darker.

Northumberland lies crafty sick, in a "worm-eaten hold of ragged stone" but the country itself is truly sick, rotten and diseased and full of dis-ease.

From Falstaff's urine and gout to the consumption of his purse to his rag-tag crew of soldiers, all Warts and Feeble, the signs point to disease. Even the tavern frequenters — Mistress Quickly and Doll Tearsheet — talk of plague and gluttony and diseases. Gloucester and Clarence, in attendance on the dying King, talk of things unnatural, "babies unholy and deformed" and nature out of order.

King Henry himself, who has "been these two weeks ill," names it:

KING HENRY IV
Then you can see the body of our kingdom
How foul it is, what rank diseases grow,
And with what danger, near the heart of it.
WARWICK
It is like a body fighting illness,
Which to his former strength may be restored
With good advice and little medicine.

King Henry, about whom this play ostensibly is, arrives late to the stage, entering at the top of Act 3. The stage direction reads *Enter KING HENRY IV in his nightgown, with a Page.* In the Festival reading, Michael Sharon as the King entered in his bare feet, which was breathtaking in its simplicity and its power, a way to show the vulnerability of the sovereign, and by extension, the nation. Magical creatures, these actors.

Over the three years of the translation process, I had the opportunity to have three different Falstaffs. Jake Hart, a big man with a big voice and a big laugh, was Falstaff in both New York workshops. During the Festival, the brilliant Lisa Wolpe, who has spent a career playing big Shakespearean roles — Iago, Hamlet, Shylock, Richard III — and directing reimagined versions of the plays (founding the Los Angeles Women's Shakespeare Company in 1993), played Falstaff in *Part 1*. She played Falstaff, she played with Hal, she played with the audience, and they ate her up, with a spoon. The next night, in *Part 2*, the great Tony Torn — himself an artistic director, with a life in both experimental and traditional theatre — wrung tears out of the same audience. Three dramatically different Falstaffs, foregrounding braggadocio, then mischief, then pathos.

I learned much from my three-year immersion in the Henrys. I learned that there was a chasm between what I thought I knew and what I actually knew, and that gap engendered all kinds of assumptions and misconceptions. In the process of discovering what I did not know, and digging into the text to transpose the incomprehensible into the comprehensible, I fell deeper in love with the language, the characters and their stories. As a result, I worked to communicate what I learned in the lines of my translations, without destroying the thing that existed first. The stated purpose of the Play On! project is to enhance the understanding of Shakespeare's plays in performance; my journey with the Henrys served that purpose for me, and my small hope is that my illumination can be shared with others who love this work as I do.

Yvette Nolan
September 2021

CHARACTERS IN THE PLAY

(in order of speaking)

RUMOR

LORD BARDOLPH

EARL OF NORTHUMBERLAND

TRAVERS, Northumberland's servant

MORTON, a messenger

SIR JOHN FALSTAFF, a knight who befriends Prince Henry

PAGE, Falstaff's page

LORD CHIEF JUSTICE

SERVANT

ARCHBISHOP OF YORK

LORD MOWBRAY, Earl Marshal

SIR RALPH HASTINGS

HOSTESS QUICKLY, mistress of the tavern

FANG, sergeant

SNARE, sergeant

GOWER, a messenger

PRINCE HENRY, King Henry's son; later King Henry V

NED POINS

BARDOLPH

LADY NORTHUMBERLAND, Northumberland's wife

LADY PERCY, Henry 'Hotspur' Percy's widow

FRANCIS, a drawer at the tavern

SECOND DRAWER

WILL, a drawer at the tavern

DOLL TEARSHEET, a prostitute

PISTOL

PETO

KING HENRY IV, King of England

EARL OF **WARWICK**

ROBERT **SHALLOW**, a country justice

SILENCE, a country justice

RALPH **MOULDY**

SIMON **SHADOW**

THOMAS **WART**

FRANCIS **FEEBLE**

PETER **BULLCALF**

EARL OF **WESTMORELAND**

PRINCE JOHN OF **LANCASTER**, King Henry IV's son

SIR JOHN **COLEVILE**

DUKE OF **GLOUCESTER**, King Henry IV's son

DUKE OF **CLARENCE**, King Henry IV's son

HARCOURT

DAVY, Shallow's servant

FIRST BEADLE

FIRST GROOM

SECOND GROOM

EPILOGUE

SIR JOHN **BLUNT** (non-speaking role)

SECOND BEADLE (non-speaking role)

Other Musicians, Lords, Servants, Officers, Soldiers, a Messenger, and a Porter

INDUCTION

Enter Rumor, painted full of tongues

RUMOR

Open your ears, for which of you will close
The vent of hearing when loud Rumor speaks?
I, from the lighted east to the drooping west,
Making the wind my post-horse, still unfold
The acts commenced on this ball of earth. 5
Upon my tongues continual slanders ride,
Which I in every language do pronounce,
Stuffing the ears of men with false reports.
I speak of peace, and smiling all the while
A secret hatred lurks to wound the world. 10
And who but Rumor, who but only I,
Scares men to muster and prepare defence
For an impending war that does not come,
Exploiting the fears of an anxious world,
That's so unsettled? Rumor is a flute 15
Blown by surmises, jealousies, conjectures
So effortlessly and so plainly played
That the blunt monster with uncounted heads,
The ever-clashing, changing multitude,
Can sound upon it. But why should I need 20
To describe myself and the way I work
To this audience? Why is Rumor here?
I run before King Harry's victory,
Who in a bloody field by Shrewsbury
Has beaten down young Hotspur and his troops, 25
Quenching the flame of bold rebellion

1

Even with the rebels' blood. But why would I
Speak so true to start? My purpose is
To spread the word that the young Prince Hal did fall
Under the wrath of noble Hotspur's sword,   30
And that the King stooped his anointed head
As low as death before the Douglas' rage.
This have I rumored through the peasant towns
Between that royal field of Shrewsbury
And this worm-eaten hold of ragged stone,   35
Where Hotspur's father, old Northumberland,
Lies crafty-sick. The messengers pour in,
And not a man of them brings other news
What they've learnt from me: false comforts brought
From Rumor's tongues wound deeper than true wrongs.   40

Exit

ACT 1 ♦ SCENE 1

Enter the Lord Bardolph at one door

LORD BARDOLPH

Who minds the gate here, hey?

Enter the Porter

Where is the Earl?

PORTER

Who shall I say you are?

LORD BARDOLPH

You tell the Earl
That the Lord Bardolph waits upon him here.   5

PORTER

His Lordship has walked out into the orchard.
If your Honour cares to knock at the gate,
Then he himself will answer.

Enter the Earl of Northumberland

2

LORD BARDOLPH

Here comes the Earl.

Porter exits

NORTHUMBERLAND

What news, Lord Bardolph? Every minute now   10

Should bring the birth of some new stratagem.

The times are wild. This conflict, like a horse

Inflamed by feed too rich, has broken loose

And tramples all before him.

LORD BARDOLPH

Noble earl,   15

I bring you certain news from Shrewsbury.

NORTHUMBERLAND

Good, God willing!

LORD BARDOLPH

As good as heart can wish.

The King is almost wounded to the death,

And thanks to the luck of my lord your son,   20

Prince Harry slain outright; and Walter Blunt

Killed by the hand of Douglas; young Prince John

And Westmoreland and Stafford fled the field;

And Falstaff, Prince Hal's beefy man Sir John,

Is prisoner to your son.   25

NORTHUMBERLAND

How do you know this?

You saw the field? You came from Shrewsbury?

LORD BARDOLPH

I spoke with one, my lord, who came from there,

A well-bred gentleman of a good name,

Who freely verified this news for me.   30

NORTHUMBERLAND

Here comes my servant Travers, whom I sent

3

On Tuesday last to seek out all the news.

Enter Travers

LORD BARDOLPH

My lord, I overtook him on the way;
And he retains no more information
Than perhaps what he has received from me.   35

NORTHUMBERLAND

Now, Travers, what good tidings come with you?

TRAVERS

My lord, a certain noble turned me back
With joyful tidings and, being better horsed,
Outrode me. After him came spurring hard
A gentleman, almost worn out with speed,   40
Who stopped by me to rest his bloodied horse.
He asked the way to Chester, and I did
Demand of him what news from Shrewsbury.
He told me that rebellion had bad luck
And that young Harry Percy's spur was cold.   45

NORTHUMBERLAND

Ha! Again:
He said young Harry Percy's spur was cold?
Of Hotspur, Coldspur? That rebellion
Had met ill luck?

LORD BARDOLPH

My lord, I'll tell you what: 50
If my young lord your son has lost the day,
Upon my honour, I'll trade my title
For a piece of lace. Never talk of it.

NORTHUMBERLAND

Why should that gentleman that rode by Travers
Give such reports then of such loss?   55

LORD BARDOLPH

Who, he?

He was some worthless fellow who's stolen

The horse he rode on and, upon my life,

Spoke capriciously.

Enter Morton

Look, here comes more news.   60

NORTHUMBERLAND

Yes, this man's brow reads like the title page,

Foretells the nature of a tragic volume.

Say, Morton, did you come from Shrewsbury?

MORTON

I ran from Shrewsbury, my noble lord,

Where hateful death put on its ugliest mask   65

To scare our party.

NORTHUMBERLAND

How does my son and brother?

You tremble, and the whiteness in your cheek

Is abler than your tongue to tell your errand.

This would you say: 'Your son did thus and thus;   70

Your brother thus; so fought the noble Douglas' —

Stopping my greedy ear with their bold deeds.

But in the end, to stop my ear indeed,

You have a sigh to blow away this praise,

Ending with 'Brother, son, and all are dead.'   75

MORTON

Douglas is living, and your brother yet,

But, for my lord your son —

NORTHUMBERLAND

Why, he is dead.

How quickly do I voice what I suspect!

The man who fears the thing he would not know   80

5

Has by instinct knowledge from others' eyes
That what he feared has happened. Yet speak, Morton.
And tell this earl his prophecy is wrong,
And I will take it as a sweet disgrace
And make you rich for doing me such wrong.   85
MORTON

You are too great for me to contradict,
Your instinct is unerring, your fears too true.
NORTHUMBERLAND

Yet, for all this, don't say that Percy's dead.
I see a loath confession in your eye.
You shake your head and think it fear or sin   90
To speak a truth. If he is slain, say so.
The tongue reports his death does not offend:
And he does sin who does deny the dead,
Not he who says the dead is not alive.
LORD BARDOLPH

I can't believe, my lord, your son is dead.   95
MORTON *(to Northumberland)*

I am sorry I should force you to believe
That which I would to God I had not seen,
But my own eyes saw him in bloody state,
Try to resist, fatigued and out of breath,
That Harry Monmouth, whose swift wrath beat down   100
The never-daunted Percy to the earth,
From where he never again would rise up.
There is much more, but in the end the news
Is that the King has won and has sent out
A speedy army to encounter you, my lord,   105
Under the command of young Lancaster
And Westmoreland. This is the sum of all.

NORTHUMBERLAND

    For this I shall have time enough to mourn.

    There is medicine in poison; if I were well,

    This news would have made me sick, but being   110

    Sick, it has in some measure made me well.

    My limbs, once weak with grief, are now enraged,

    Three times stronger. Away, you feeble crutch!

(he throws down his crutch)

    A scaly gauntlet now with joints of steel

    Must glove this hand. Away, you patient's cap.   115

    Now bind my brows with iron, and approach

    The roughest hour that time and spite dare bring

    To frown upon enraged Northumberland.

    Let the heavens fall! Release the oceans

    From mother Nature's grip. Let order die,   120

    And let this world no longer be a stage

    On which to strut a lengthy final act.

    Let the ill spirit of the firstborn Cain

    Reign in all bosoms, that, each heart being set

    On bloodshed, this murderous play may end,   125

    And darkness be the burier of the dead.

MORTON

    Sweet earl, divorce not wisdom from your honor.

    The lives of all your loyal confederates

    Depend on you; your health, if you succumb

    To stormy passion, must likewise decay.   130

    You conjured up the war, my noble lord,

    And calculated risk, before you said,

    'Let's raise a force.' You knew there was a chance

    That in the rain of blows your son might drop.

    You knew he straddled perils, on an edge,   135

    More likely to fall in than overleap.

You were warned his flesh was susceptible
To wounds and scars and that his eager spirit
Would lead him where the greatest danger lay.
Yet you did say 'Go forth.'   140

LORD BARDOLPH

We all that are affected by this loss
Knew that we ventured on such dangerous seas,
The odds of our survival, ten to one;
And yet we ventured, for what should be feared
Paled when compared to that which could be gained;   145
And since we are undone, venture again.
Come, we will gamble all, body and goods.

MORTON

It's more than time — And, my most noble lord,
I hear for certain, and do speak the truth:
The noble Archbishop of York has raised   150
A well-appointed army. But now he
Uses men's faith to spur rebellion.
Supposed sincere and holy in his thoughts,
He's followed both with body and with mind,
And does inflame his soldiers with the blood   155
Of fair King Richard, spilled on Pomfret stones;
Derives from heaven his quarrel and his cause;
Tells them he does defend a bleeding land,
Gasping for life under great Bolingbroke;
And men from every walk do follow him.   160

NORTHUMBERLAND

I knew of this before, but, to speak truth,
This present grief had wiped it from my mind.
Go in with me and let us rouse each man
The surest way for safety and revenge.
Send messengers with letters, and with speed.   165

Never so few, and never yet more need.

They exit

ACT 1 ◆ SCENE 2

LONDON, A STREET

Enter Sir John Falstaff, with his Page bearing his sword and buckler

FALSTAFF

Fellow, you runt, what says the doctor about my water?

PAGE

He said, sir, the water itself was a good healthy water, but, for the party that owned it, he might have more diseases than he knew of.

FALSTAFF

Men of all sorts take pride in jeering at me. The brain of this 5 foolish-compounded clay, man, is not able to invent anything that inspires laughter more than I invent, or is invented on me. I am not only witty in myself, but the cause of wit in other men. I walk here before you like a sow that has crushed all but one of her litter. If the prince put you into my service 10 for any other reason than to irritate me, why then I have no sense at all. You wretched sprout, you are fitter to be worn in my cap than to wait at my heels. I've never been served by a trinket before, but I will inset you in neither gold nor silver, but in ragged clothes, and send you back again to your mas- 15 ter as a jewel. The juvenile, the Prince your master, whose chin is not yet downy — I will sooner have a beard grow in the palm of my hand than he shall get one on his cheek, and yet he'll be crowing as if he's been a man ever since his father was a bachelor. What did Master Dommelton say about the 20 satin for my short cloak and my long pants?

PAGE

He said, sir, you should procure him a better guarantee than

Bardolph. He would not take his bond nor yours. He has no faith in the security.

FALSTAFF

Let him be damned like the glutton! A wretched traitor, a 25
rascally yes-man trader, to lead a gentleman along and then insist upon security! I'd as soon they'd put poison in my mouth as offer to stop it with 'security.' I expected him to have sent me two dozen yards of satin, as I am a true knight, and he sends me 'security.' 30

Enter the Lord Chief Justice and Servant

PAGE

Sir, here comes the nobleman that had the Prince imprisoned for striking him about Bardolph.

FALSTAFF

Wait, hide; I will not see him.

They begin to exit

CHIEF JUSTICE

Who's he that goes there?

SERVANT

Falstaff, if it please your lordship. 35

CHIEF JUSTICE

He that was investigated for the robbery?

SERVANT

He, my lord: but he has since done good service at Shrewsbury, and, as I hear, now leads some soldiers to the Lord John of Lancaster.

CHIEF JUSTICE

What, to York? Call him back again. 40

SERVANT

Sir John Falstaff!

FALSTAFF

Boy, tell him I am deaf.

ACT 1 ♦ SCENE 2

PAGE

You must speak louder. My master is deaf.

CHIEF JUSTICE

I am sure he is, to any thing that does him no good — Go,
pluck him by the elbow. I must speak with him.   45

SERVANT *(plucking Falstaff's sleeve)*

Sir John!

FALSTAFF

What, a young rogue and begging? Are there not wars? Is
there not employment? Does the King not lack subjects? Do
the rebels not need soldiers?

SERVANT

You mistake me, sir.   50

FALSTAFF

Why, sir, did I say you were an honest man? Setting my
knighthood and my soldiership aside, I'd be a lowdown liar
if I had said so.

SERVANT

Well then, sir, set your knighthood and your soldiership
aside, and permit me to tell you, you are a lowdown liar if   55
you say I am anything but an honest man.

FALSTAFF

I permit you tell me so? I lay aside that which is integral to
me? If I permit you anything, hang me; if you take permis-
sion, you had better be hanged. You're barking up the wrong
tree. Away! Be gone!   60

SERVANT

Sir, my lord would speak with you.

CHIEF JUSTICE

Sir John Falstaff, a word with you.

FALSTAFF

My good lord. God give your Lordship good time of day. I

11

am glad to see your lordship about. I heard tell your Lordship was sick. I hope your Lordship goes about on doctor's   65
advice. Your Lordship, though not clean past your youth, has
yet some touch of fever in you, some knowledge of the fleet-
ing nature of time in you, and I must humbly beseech your
Lordship to take better care of your health.

CHIEF JUSTICE

Sir John, I sent for you before your expedition to Shrewsbury.   70

FALSTAFF

If it please your Lordship, I hear his Majesty is returned with
some discomfort from Wales.

CHIEF JUSTICE

I am not talking about his Majesty. You would not come
when I sent for you.

FALSTAFF

And I hear, moreover, his Highness is fallen into this same   75
wretched apoplexy.

CHIEF JUSTICE

Well, God mend him. I beg you let me speak with you.

FALSTAFF

This apoplexy, as I understand it, is a kind of lethargy, if
it please your Lordship, a kind of sleeping in the blood, a
wretched tingling.   80

CHIEF JUSTICE

Why are you telling me about it? It is what it is.

FALSTAFF

It stems from much grief, from study, and from perturbation
of the brain. I have read the cause of his effects in the schol-
ars. It is a kind of deafness.

CHIEF JUSTICE

I think you have contracted the disease, for you don't hear   85
what I say to you.

FALSTAFF

Very likely, my lord, very likely. Rather, if it please you, it is
the disease of not listening, the affliction of inattention, that
I am troubled with.

CHIEF JUSTICE

To shackle you by the ankles would correct the attention of   90
your ears, and I do not mind becoming your physician. I sent
for you, when you were charged with crimes that could cost
you your life, to come speak with me.

FALSTAFF

I was then advised by my learned counsel that since I was in
military service, I need not come.   95

CHIEF JUSTICE

Well, the truth is, Sir John, you live in great infamy.

FALSTAFF

He that buckles himself in my belt cannot live in less.

CHIEF JUSTICE

Your means are very slender, and your waste is great.

FALSTAFF

I would it were otherwise. I would my means were greater,
and my waist slenderer.   100

CHIEF JUSTICE

You have misled the youthful prince.

FALSTAFF

The young prince has misled me. I am the fellow with the
great belly, and he my dog.

CHIEF JUSTICE

Well, I am loath to aggravate a new-healed wound. Your day's
service at Shrewsbury has somewhat brightened your night's   105
exploit at Gad's hill. You may thank the turbulent times for
your escaping the consequences of that action.

FALSTAFF

My lord?

CHIEF JUSTICE

But since all is well, keep it so. Do not wake a sleeping wolf.

FALSTAFF

To wake a wolf is as bad as to smell a rat. 110

CHIEF JUSTICE

Oh, you are like a candle, the better part burnt out.

FALSTAFF

A holiday candle made of tallow, my lord, wanes. But I'm more of the waxing type, as my growth demonstrates.

CHIEF JUSTICE

Every white hair on your face should effect in you some gravity.

FALSTAFF

Effect of gravy, gravy, gravy. 115

CHIEF JUSTICE

You follow the young prince up and down, like his bad angel.

FALSTAFF

Not so, my lord. Your bad angel is light, and he that looks on me would see that I am weighty. And yet, in some respects, I cannot disagree. I can no longer tell. Virtue is of so little regard in these mercenary times that true valour is turned 120 ringmaster; intelligence is made a tapster, and her quick wit is wasted in tallying bar-bills. You who are old do not consider the capacities of we who are young.

CHIEF JUSTICE

Do you set down your name in the scroll of youth, you who has age written all over him? Do you not have a moist eye, a 125 dry hand? A yellow cheek, a white beard, a decreasing leg, an increasing belly? Is your voice not broken, your wind short, your chin double, your wit single, and every part of you blasted with antiquity? And will you yet call yourself young?

Shame, shame, shame, Sir John.   130

FALSTAFF

My lord, I was born about three o'clock in the afternoon, with
a white head and something of a round belly. For my voice,
I have lost it with hollering and singing of drinking songs.
I will not attempt to prove my youth further, I will not. The
truth is, I am only old in judgement and understanding. And   135
he that will caper with me for a thousand pounds, let him
lend me the money, and have at it. For the box of the ear that
the Prince gave you, he gave it like a rude prince, and you
took it like a refined lord. I have chastised him for it, and the
young lion repents.   140
(Aside) Mind you, not in ashes and sackcloth, but in new silk
and old sack.

CHIEF JUSTICE

Well, God send the prince a better companion.

FALSTAFF

God send the companion a better prince. I cannot rid my
hands of him.   145

CHIEF JUSTICE

Well, the King has separated you and Prince Harry. I hear
you are going with Lord John of Lancaster against the Archbishop and the Earl of Northumberland.

FALSTAFF

Yes, I thank your pretty sweet wit for it. But all of you that
kiss my Lady Peace at home, pray that our armies do not   150
meet in hot battle, for, by God, I take only two shirts with me,
and I do not intend to sweat profusely. If it is a hot day and I
brandish any thing but a bottle, I'll never drink again. There
is not a dangerous action can peep his head out but I am sent
to deal with it. Well, I cannot live forever. But that is always   155
the way with our English nation, if they have a good thing,

to overuse it. Since you insist on saying I am an old man, you should give me rest. I would to God the enemy was not so terrified of me. I'd rather sit and grow rust than be ground to nothing with perpetual motion.   160

CHIEF JUSTICE

Well, be honest, be honest, and God bless your expedition.

FALSTAFF

Will your lordship lend me a thousand pounds so that I may supply it?

CHIEF JUSTICE

Not a penny, not a penny. You are too impatient to bear crosses. Farewell. Commend me to my cousin Westmoreland.   165

Lord Chief Justice and his Servant exit

FALSTAFF

Boy!

PAGE

Sir.

FALSTAFF

What money is in my purse?

PAGE

Seven nickels and two pennies.

FALSTAFF

I can get no remedy for this consumption of the purse. Bor-   170
rowing only prolongs and prolongs it, but the disease is incurable. Go bear this letter to my Lord of Lancaster, this to the Prince, this to the Earl of Westmoreland, and this to old Mistress Ursula, whom I have sworn weekly to marry since I found the first white hair on my chin. Get to it. You know   175
where to find me.

Exit Page

A pox on this gout! Or a gout on this pox, for it's one or the other that makes my great toe hurt like hell. Doesn't matter if

I do limp. I can blame it on the wars, and justify my pension.
A good wit will make use of any thing. I will turn diseases to   180
my advantage.

He exits

ACT 1 ♦ SCENE 3

YORK, THE ARCHBISHOP'S PALACE

Enter the Archbishop of York, Thomas Mowbray (Earl Marshal),
the Lord Hastings, and Lord Bardolph

ARCHBISHOP OF YORK

Now you have heard our cause and known our means,
And, my most noble friends, I pray you all
Speak plainly your opinions of our hopes.
Lord Mowbray first, what do you say to it?

MOWBRAY

I understand the need to take up arms,   5
But still I would be better satisfied
To know what means we use to grow our strength
To be equipped both bold and big enough
To meet the might and power of the King.

HASTINGS

Our present muster grows to swell the ranks   10
To five-and-twenty thousand first-class men;
Our reinforcements largely do depend
On great Northumberland, whose bosom burns
With an incensed fire of injuries.

LORD BARDOLPH

The question then, Lord Hastings, must be this;   15
Whether our present five and twenty thousand
May well succeed without Northumberland.

HASTINGS

With him we may.

LORD BARDOLPH

Yes, truly, there's the point.

But if without him we are thought too feeble,   20

My judgement is, we should not step too far

Till we have his assistance close at hand.

For in a fight so bloody-faced as this

Conjecture, expectation, and desire

For doubtful aid should not be counted on.   25

ARCHBISHOP OF YORK

It's very true, Lord Bardolph, for indeed

That was young Hotspur's case at Shrewsbury.

LORD BARDOLPH

It was, my lord; he buoyed himself with hope,

Having faith in the promise of supply,

Awaiting the arrival of an army   30

That proved to be much smaller than he thought,

And so, with great imagination

Common to madmen, led his powers to death

And, blindly, leapt into destruction.

HASTINGS

But still, my lord, it never hurts to map   35

The plans and paths to possible success.

LORD BARDOLPH

But it can hurt, if plans we make for war —

Denying what the actual conditions —

Live so in hope as in an early spring

Are buds tricked into blooming; in which case   40

Hope gives not so much promise as despair

That frost will bite them.

HASTINGS

Say that our hopes, which could be realised,

Were not fulfilled, and that we now command

As big a force as it will ever be,   45
I think our army now is strong enough,
Even as we are, to stand against the King.

LORD BARDOLPH

The King has only five-and-twenty thousand?

HASTINGS

Against us yes, and perhaps less, Lord Bardolph,
For his divisions, in these times of war,   50
Are in three parts: one power against the French,
And one against Glendower, which means a third
Opposes us. So is the infirm king
In three divided, and his coffers sound
With hollow poverty and emptiness.   55

ARCHBISHOP OF YORK

That he should draw his several strengths together
And come against us in full power
Need not to be dreaded.

HASTINGS

If he should do so,
He leaves his back unarmed, the French and Welsh   60
Baying right at his heels. Never fear that.

LORD BARDOLPH

Who is it likely leads his force against us?

HASTINGS

The Duke of Lancaster and Westmoreland;
Against the Welsh, himself and Harry Monmouth;
But who is delegated against the French   65
I cannot know for sure.

ARCHBISHOP OF YORK

Let us move on,
And tell the people why we take up arms.
The commonwealth is sick of their own choice.

Their over-greedy love has surfeited. 70
Foundation built upon the vulgar heart
Will always be both giddy and unsure.
Oh foolish mob, with what loud applause
Did you beat heaven with blessing Bolingbroke
Before he was what you would have him be. 75
And being now dressed in your own desires,
You, beastly feeder, are so full of him
That you provoke yourself to heave him up.
So, so, you common dog, did you disgorge
Your greedy stomach of the royal Richard, 80
And now you would eat your dead vomit up
And howl to find it. What trust is in these times?
They who, when Richard lived, would have him die
Have now become impassioned on his grave.
You, that threw dust upon his goodly head 85
When through proud London he came sighing on
At the feet of admired Bolingbroke,
Now cry 'Oh earth, give us that king again,
And take back this!' Oh thoughts of men are cursed!
Past and future seem best; the present worst. 90

MOWBRAY

Shall we go now assemble and set on?

HASTINGS

We are time's subjects, time bids us be gone.

They exit

ACT 2 ♦ SCENE 1

LONDON, A STREET

Enter Hostess Quickly, of the tavern, with two officers,
Fang, and Snare, who lags behind

HOSTESS

Master Fang, have you filed the suit?

FANG

It is filed.

HOSTESS

Where's your assistant? Is he a gutsy assistant? Will he fight
with vigour?

FANG

— Mister — where's Snare?   5

HOSTESS

Oh Lord, yes, good Master Snare.

SNARE

Here, here.

FANG

Snare, we must arrest Sir John Falstaff.

HOSTESS

Yes, good Master Snare, I have filed suit and all.

SNARE

It could cost some of us our lives, for he will stab.   10

HOSTESS

Unlucky day, take heed of him. He stabbed me in my own
house, and that most beastly, in good faith. He does not care
what mischief he does. If his weapon's out, he will thrust like
any devil. He will spare neither man, woman, nor child.

FANG

If I can grapple with him, I don't care about his thrust. 15

HOSTESS

No, neither do I. I'll be at your elbow.

FANG

If I but fist him once, if he comes within my reach —

HOSTESS

I am undone by his going. I warrant you, he's an infinitive drain upon my resources. Good Master Fang, hold him sure. Good Master Snare, do not let him escape. I beg you, since 20 my action is entered and my case so openly known to the world, let him be brought in to answer for it. A hundred pounds is a big weight for a poor lone woman to bear: and I have borne, and borne, and borne, and have been fobbed off, and fobbed off, and fobbed off, from this day to that day, 25 that it is a shame to think of it. There is no honesty in such dealing, unless a woman should be made an ass and a beast to bear every rogue's wrong. Here he comes, and that errant Madeira-nosed knave, Bardolph, with him. Do your duties, do your duties, Master Fang and Master Snare, do me, do me, 30 do me your duties.

Enter Falstaff, Page, and Bardolph

FALSTAFF

How now, what's up? What's the matter?

FANG

Sir John, I arrest you at the suit of Mistress Quickly.

FALSTAFF

Away, scoundrels! — Draw, Bardolph! Cut off the villain's head. Throw the wench in the channel. 35

HOSTESS

Throw me in the channel! I'll throw you in the channel. Will you, will you, you bastardly rogue? — Murder, murder!

22

FALSTAFF

Beat them off, Bardolph.

FANG

A rescue, a rescue!

HOSTESS

Good people, bring a rescue or two — You will, will you? You will, will you? Do, do, you rogue! Do, you rotter!   40

FALSTAFF

Away, you lowlife, you scoundrel, you frump! I'll paddle your posterior.

Enter the Lord Chief Justice, and his men

CHIEF JUSTICE

What is the matter? Keep the peace here, hear?!

HOSTESS

My good lord, be good to me. I beseech you stand up for me.   45

CHIEF JUSTICE

Well now, Sir John! What, are you brawling here?

Does this become your place, your age and business?

You should have been well on your way to York. —

Stand away from him, fellow. Why do you hang onto him?

HOSTESS

Oh my most worshipful lord, if it please your Grace, I am a   50 poor widow of Eastcheap, and he is arrested at my suit.

CHIEF JUSTICE

For what sum?

HOSTESS

It is more than for some, my lord; it is for all, all I have. He has eaten me out of house and home. He has put all my substance into that fat belly of his. *(to Falstaff)* But I will have   55 some of it out again, or I will ride you nights like the mare.

FALSTAFF

I think I am as likely to ride the mare if I have the opportunity to mount up.

CHIEF JUSTICE

What goes on here, Sir John? Shame, what man of good tem- per would endure this uproar? Are you not ashamed to force 60 a poor widow to so rough a course to come by what is hers?

FALSTAFF

What is the gross sum that I owe you?

HOSTESS

Truly, if you were an honest man, yourself and the money too. You did swear to me upon a gold-lined goblet, sitting in my Dolphin chamber, at the round table, by a coal fire, upon 65 Wednesday in Whitsun week, when the Prince broke your head for suggesting his father was a charlatan, you did swear to me then, as I was washing your wound, to marry me and make me my lady your wife. Can you deny it? Did not Missus Keech, the butcher's wife, come in then and call me Gossip 70 Quickly. And did you not, when she was gone down stairs, reproach me to be less familiar with such poor people, saying that before long they would call me madam? And did you not kiss me and bid me fetch you thirty shillings? I ask you now to swear on the Bible. Deny it, if you can. 75

FALSTAFF

My lord, this is a poor mad soul, and she says all through the town that her eldest son looks like you. She has been well-off, and the truth is, poverty has made her mad. As to these fool- ish officers, I beg you allow me redress against them.

CHIEF JUSTICE

Sir John, Sir John, I am well acquainted with your manner 80 of wrenching the true cause the false way. You have, as it appears to me, manipulated the easy-yielding spirit of this woman, and made her serve your uses both in purse and in person.

HOSTESS

Yes, in truth, my lord.   85

CHIEF JUSTICE

Hush, now. — Pay her the debt you owe her, and remedy the
villainy you have done to her. One you may do with sterling
money, and the other with genuine repentance.

FALSTAFF

My lord, I will not undergo this rebuke without reply. You
call honorable boldness 'insolent disrespect.' If a man bows   90
and says nothing, he is virtuous. No, my lord, my respect for
you notwithstanding, I will not be your supplicant. I say to
you, I wish to be released from these officers, as I have urgent
business on behalf of the King.

CHIEF JUSTICE

You speak as if you can do no wrong; but defend the honor of   95
your reputation, and satisfy this poor woman.

FALSTAFF

Come here, hostess.

He speaks aside to the Hostess

Enter Gower

CHIEF JUSTICE

Now, Master Gower, what news?

GOWER

The king, my lord, and Harry Prince of Wales
Are near at hand. The rest this letter tells.   100

FALSTAFF *(to the Hostess)*

As I am a gentleman!

HOSTESS

By god, you've said so before.

FALSTAFF

As I am a gentleman. Come. No more words about it.

HOSTESS

By this heavenly ground I tread on, I must resign myself
to pawning both my dishes and the tapestry of my dining 105
chambers.

FALSTAFF

Glasses, glasses are the only things for drinking: and as for
your walls, a pretty slight trifle, or the story of the Prodigal
or the German hunting in watercolours is worth a thousand
of these bed-curtains and these moth-eaten tapestries. Loan 110
me ten pounds, if you can. Come, if it were not for your
moodiness, there'd be no better wench in England. Go, wash
your face, and withdraw the suit. Come, you must not be in
this humour with me. Do you not know me? Come, come. I
know you were put up to this. 115

HOSTESS

Please, Sir John, let me have but a few pounds. Honestly, I am
loath to pawn my dishes, so God save me, la!

FALSTAFF

Never mind. I'll try elsewhere. You'll always be a fool.

HOSTESS

Well, you shall have it, though I pawn my gown. I hope you'll
come to supper. You'll pay me everything? 120

FALSTAFF

Will I live?

(to Bardolph)

Go, with her, with her. Stay close, stay close.

HOSTESS

Will you have Doll Tearsheet meet you at supper?

FALSTAFF

No more words. Let's have her.

Hostess, Fang, Snare, Bardolph, Page, and others exit

CHIEF JUSTICE *(to Gower)*

I have heard better news. 125

FALSTAFF *(to Chief Justice)*

What's the news, my lord?

CHIEF JUSTICE *(to Gower)*

Where did the King stay last night?

GOWER

At Basingstoke, my lord.

FALSTAFF *(to Chief Justice)*

I hope, my lord, all's well. What is the news, my lord?

CHIEF JUSTICE *(to Gower)*

Do all his forces return? 130

GOWER

No. Fifteen hundred foot, five hundred horse,

Are marching to my Lord of Lancaster,

Against Northumberland and the Archbishop.

FALSTAFF *(to Chief Justice)*

The King comes back from Wales, my noble lord?

CHIEF JUSTICE *(to Gower)*

You shall have letters from me presently. 135

Come. Go along with me, good Master Gower.

FALSTAFF

My lord!

CHIEF JUSTICE

What's the matter?

FALSTAFF

Master Gower, can I entreat you to dine with me?

GOWER

I must wait upon my good lord here. I thank you, good Sir 140
John.

CHIEF JUSTICE

Sir John, you loiter here too long, seeing you are to recruit soldiers in counties as you go.

FALSTAFF

Will you dine with me, Master Gower?

CHIEF JUSTICE

What foolish master taught you these manners, Sir John? 145

FALSTAFF

Master Gower, if they do not become me, he was a fool who taught them to me. — This is how a fencing match is played, my lord: tap for tap, and then we are done.

CHIEF JUSTICE

May the Lord enlighten you! You are a great fool.

They separate and exit

ACT 2 ◆ SCENE 2

LONDON, ANOTHER STREET

Enter the Prince and Poins

PRINCE HENRY

By God, I am exceedingly weary.

POINS

Has it come to that? I thought that weariness did not dare affect one of such high blood.

PRINCE HENRY

Honestly, it does me, though it does diminish my dignity to acknowledge it. Should I be ashamed that I crave a light beer? 5

POINS

Why, a prince should not be so poorly brought up that he displays such low tastes.

PRINCE HENRY

It's likely then my appetite is not a princely one, for, I swear, I am thinking only of the poor creature, light beer. But, indeed, these humble considerations do distance me from 10 my station. What a disgrace it is that I remember your name!

or that I will know your face tomorrow.

POINS

Tell me, how many good young princes would do so, their fathers being as sick as yours is at this time?

PRINCE HENRY

Shall I tell you one thing, Poins?   15

POINS

Go on. I can withstand whatever thing that you will tell me.

PRINCE HENRY

Indeed, I tell you, it would be unseemly for me to be sad, now that my father is sick — although I could tell you, as one whom I call friend, for lack of a better — I could be sad, and very sad indeed too.   20

POINS

Very difficult on such a subject.

PRINCE HENRY

By god, you think me as disgraceful as you and Falstaff for obduracy and persistency. Let the end judge the man. But I tell you, my heart bleeds inwardly that my father is so sick; and the consequence of keeping such vile company as you   25 has prevented all display of sorrow.

POINS

The reason?

PRINCE HENRY

What would you think of me, if I should weep?

POINS

I would think you a most royal hypocrite.

PRINCE HENRY

And so would every man, and you are a blessed fellow to   30 think as every man thinks: no man's thought in the world strays less from the prevailing wisdom than yours. Every man would think me a hypocrite indeed. And what is it that inspires in you this judgement?

POINS

Why, because you have been so lewd and so closely bound   35
to Falstaff.

PRINCE HENRY

And to you.

POINS

Actually, I am well spoken of. I hear it with my own ears. The
worst that they can say of me is that I am a poor penniless
second brother and that I am good in a fight; and those two   40
things, I confess, I cannot help. By god, here comes Bardolph.

Enter Bardolph and Page

PRINCE HENRY

And the boy that I gave Falstaff. He had him from me
civilised, and it looks like the fat villain has transformed him
into ape.

BARDOLPH

God save your grace!   45

PRINCE HENRY

And yours, most noble Bardolph!

POINS

Come, you virtuous ass, you bashful fool, must you be blush-
ing? Why do you blush now? What a maidenly man-at-arms
have you become! Is it so difficult to knock off a pot of ale?

PAGE

He called me just now, my lord, through a red lattice, and I   50
could not tell his face from the window. At last I spied his
eyes, and I thought he had made two holes in the ale-wife's
new petticoat and so peeped through.

PRINCE HENRY

See how the boy has benefited?

BARDOLPH

Away, you wretched upright rabbit, away!   55

POINS

Oh, that this good blossom could be kept from canker-
worms! Well, there is sixpence to preserve you.

He gives the Page money

BARDOLPH

If you do not get him hanged, the gallows shall be robbed.

PRINCE HENRY

And how does your master, Bardolph?

BARDOLPH

Well, my lord. He heard of your Grace's coming to town.   60
There's a letter for you.

POINS

Delivered with all due respect. And how is your master, the
sweet beef?

BARDOLPH

In bodily health, sir.

POINS

Truly, the immortal part needs a physician, but he does not   65
care. Although it's sick, it does not die.

PRINCE HENRY

I do allow this lump to be as familiar with me as my dog, and
he knows it, for look how he writes.

POINS *(reads)*

John Falstaff, knight. He has to tell everyone that, every
opportunity he has to name himself, just like those who   70
are kin to the King, for they never prick their finger without saying, 'There's some of the King's blood spilt.' 'What do
you mean?' the unsuspecting observer says. The answer is as
ready as a borrower's cap: 'I am the King's poor cousin, sir.'

31

PRINCE HENRY

No, they will be kin to us, even if they have to trace it back 75
to the beginning of time. But to the letter. *(reads) Sir John
Falstaff, knight, to the son of the King, nearest his father, Harry
Prince of Wales, greeting.*

POINS

Why, this is a decree.

PRINCE HENRY

Hush! 80

(Prince reads)

I will imitate the honourable Romans in brevity.

POINS

Surely he means brevity in breath, short-winded.

PRINCE HENRY *(reads)*

*I commend me to you, I commend you, and I leave you. Be not
too familiar with Poins, for he misuses your favours so much
that he swears you are to marry his sister Nell. Repent at idle* 85
*times as you may, and so, farewell. Yours, up and down, which
is as much as to say, as you use him,*
Jack Falstaff with my familiars,
John with my brothers and sisters,
and Sir John with all Europe. 90

POINS

My lord, I'll steep this letter in sack and make him eat it.

PRINCE HENRY

That's to make him eat twenty of his words. But do you use
me as he says, Ned? Must I marry your sister?

POINS

God send the wench such good luck! But I never said so.

PRINCE HENRY

Well, we are wasting time, and the spirits of the wise sit in the 95
clouds and mock us. Is your master here in London?

BARDOLPH

Yes, my lord.

PRINCE HENRY

Where does he dine? Does the old boar feed at the old pigsty?

BARDOLPH

At the old place, my lord, in Eastcheap.

PRINCE HENRY

Does he have company? 100

PAGE

The usual companions, my lord.

PRINCE HENRY

Do any women dine with him?

PAGE

None, my lord, except for old Mistress Quickly and Mistress Doll Tearsheet.

PRINCE HENRY

What harlot is that? 105

PAGE

A respectable gentlewoman, sir, and a relation of my master's.

PRINCE HENRY

The kind of relations the parish heifers are to the town bull.

— Shall we spy upon them, Ned, at supper?

POINS

I am your shadow, my lord. I'll follow you.

PRINCE HENRY

Mister — you boy — and Bardolph, no word to your master 110
that I am already in town. There's for your silence.

BARDOLPH

I have no tongue, sir.

PAGE

And for mine, sir, I will govern it.

33

PRINCE HENRY

Farewell. Go.

Bardolph and Page exit

This Doll Tearsheet must be as common as the road. 115

POINS

No doubt, as common as the way between Saint
Alban's and London.

PRINCE HENRY

How might we see Falstaff show his true colours tonight, and
not be seen ourselves?

POINS

Put on aprons, and wait on him at his table as servers. 120

PRINCE HENRY

From prince to apprentice: a low transformation that I will
undertake, for in every action the purpose must match the
folly. Follow me, Ned.

They exit

ACT 2 ◆ SCENE 3

WARKWORTH, BEFORE THE CASTLE

Enter Northumberland, Lady Northumberland, and Lady Percy

NORTHUMBERLAND

I ask you, loving wife, and gentle daughter,
Support me in my arduous affairs.
Do not reflect a grim face of the times
And be, like them, so troublesome to me.

LADY NORTHUMBERLAND

I have given up. I will speak no more. 5
Do what you will; your wisdom be your guide.

NORTHUMBERLAND

Alas, sweet wife, my honour is at risk,
And nothing can redeem it but my going.

34

LADY PERCY

    Oh yet, for God's sake, go not to these wars.
    The time was, father, that you broke your word,   10
    When you were more obliged to it than now,
    When your own Percy, when my heart's dear Harry,
    Threw many a northward look to see his father
    Come with his powers; but he did long in vain.
    Who then persuaded you to stay at home?   15
    Two honors were lost there, yours and your son's.
    For yours, may God in heaven brighten it.
    For his, it clung to him as does the sun
    To the grey vault of heaven, and by his light
    Was all the chivalry of England moved   20
    To do brave acts. He was indeed the glass
    In which the noble youth did dress themselves.
    In speech, in gait, in diet, in delight,
    In military rules, humours of blood,
    He was the mark and glass, copy and book,   25
    That influenced others. And him — Oh wondrous him!
    Oh miracle of men! — him did you leave,
    Second to none, unseconded by you,
    To look upon the hideous god of war
    So disadvantaged, to face in battle   30
    With nothing but the sound of his own name
    Left to defend himself. So you left him.
    Never, oh never, do his ghost the wrong
    To act as if your honor matters more
    With others than with him. Let them do it.   35
    Lord Mowbray and the Archbishop are strong.
    Had my sweet Harry had but half their numbers,
    Today I might be hanging on his neck,
    Speaking of Prince Hal's grave.

NORTHUMBERLAND

    For heaven's sake, 40

    Fair daughter, you do drive my spirits downwards

    Lamenting once again my past mistakes.

    But I must go and meet with danger there,

    Or it will seek me in another place

    And find me even less prepared. 45

LADY NORTHUMBERLAND

    Oh, fly to Scotland,

    Until the nobles and their new raised forces

    Have had a little taste of the King's strength.

LADY PERCY

    If they can take advantage of the King,

    Then you join with them, like a rib of steel, 50

    To make strength stronger; but, for all our loves,

    First let them try themselves. So did your son;

    He was so tested. So I am a widow,

    And never will my life be long enough

    To rain upon remembrance with my eyes, 55

    That it may grow and sprout as high as heaven,

    To pay a tribute to my noble husband.

NORTHUMBERLAND

    Come, come, go in with me. My mind's as full

    As when the tide swells up unto its height,

    It makes it seem like time is standing still. 60

    Gladly I'd go to meet the Archbishop,

    But many thousand reasons hold me back.

    I will commit to Scotland. There I'll be

    'Til the right time and opportunity.

They exit

ACT 2 ◆ SCENE 4

LONDON, THE BOAR'S-HEAD TAVERN IN EASTCHEAP

Enter two Drawers

FRANCIS

What the devil have you brought there — applejohns? You know that Sir John cannot stand an applejohn.

SECOND DRAWER

God's honest truth. The Prince once set a dish of applejohns before him and told him there were five more Sir Johns and, doffing his hat, said 'I will now take my leave of these six dry, 5 round, old, withered knights.' It angered Sir John to the core. But he is over it.

FRANCIS

Why then, lay the cloth, and set them down, and see if you can find Sneak's musicians. Mistress Tearsheet would like to hear some music. 10

Enter Will

WILL

Mister, the Prince and Master Poins will be in shortly, and they will put on two of our jackets and aprons, and Sir John must not know of it. Bardolph has brought word.

SECOND DRAWER

By god, this will be great fun. It will be an excellent jest.

FRANCIS

I'll see if I can find Sneak. 15

Exits with the Second Drawer
Enter Hostess and Doll Tearsheet

HOSTESS

Truly, sweetheart, I think now you are in an excellent good temporality. Your pulsidge beats as extraordinarily as a heart would desire, and your colour, I wager, is as red as any rose, in good truth, la. But, truly, you have drunk too much

37

Canary wine, and that's marvellous penetrating wine, and it   20
perfumes the blood before one can say 'What's this?' How are
you doing now?

DOLL TEARSHEET

Better than I was. Hem.

HOSTESS

Why, that's well said. A good heart's worth gold. Lo, here
comes Sir John.   25

Enter Falstaff

FALSTAFF *(singing)*

'When Arthur first in court,'

(to Will)

Empty the chamber pot.

Will exits

(singing)

— 'And was a worthy king' —
How goes it, Mistress Doll?

DOLL TEARSHEET

A plague on you, you dirty rascal.   30

FALSTAFF

You make rascals fat, Mistress Doll.

DOLL TEARSHEET

I make them? Gluttony and diseases make them; I don't
make them.

FALSTAFF

If the cook helps to make gluttony, you help to make diseases,
Doll. We catch it from you, Doll, we catch it from you.   35

DOLL TEARSHEET

Yes, joy, our chains and our jewels.

FALSTAFF

Your broaches, pearls, and gems — for to serve bravely is to
come limping off, you know: to come off the breach with his

pike bent bravely, and to surgery bravely; to venture to the
loaded chambers bravely —   40

DOLL TEARSHEET

Hang yourself, you muddy eel, hang yourself!

HOSTESS

I swear, here we go again. You two never meet but you fall
to some discord. Truth be told, you are both as rheumatic as
two dry toasts. You cannot bear one another's confirmities.
What the devil! One must bear, and that must be you. You are 45
the weaker vessel, as they say, the emptier vessel.

DOLL TEARSHEET

Can a weak empty vessel bear such a huge full barrel? There's
a whole merchant's venture of Bordeaux stuffed in him. You
have not seen a ship better stuffed in the hold. — Come, I'll
be friends with you, Jack. You are going to the wars, and   50
whether I shall ever see you again or no, nobody cares.

Enter Drawer

SECOND DRAWER

Sir, Ancient Pistol's below and would speak with you.

DOLL TEARSHEET

Hang him, swaggering rascal! Don't let him come here. He is
the foulest-mouthed rogue in England.

HOSTESS

If he swaggers, don't let him come here. No, by god, I must   55
live among my neighbours. I'll have no swaggerers here. I
have a good name with the very best. Shut the door. There
will be no swaggerers here. I have not lived all this while, to
have swaggering now. Shut the door, please.

FALSTAFF

Do you hear, hostess?   60

HOSTESS

Calm yourself, Sir John. There will be no swaggerers here.

FALSTAFF

Do you hear? It is my ensign.

HOSTESS

Oh for heaven's sake, Sir John, I don't want to hear it. And
your ancient swaggerer will not come through my doors. No,
I'll have no swaggerers here.   65

FALSTAFF

He's no swaggerer, hostess; a tame cheater, I swear. You may
stroke him as gently as a puppy greyhound. Call him up,
waiter.

Exit Drawer

HOSTESS

'Cheater' you call him? I will bar no honest man from my
house, nor no cheater. But I do not love swaggering. I swear,   70
I get all agitated, when one says 'swagger.' Feel, masters, how
I shake; look, I'm telling you.

DOLL TEARSHEET

So you do, hostess.

HOSTESS

Do I? Yes, in very truth, do I, as if I were an aspen leaf. I cannot abide swaggerers.   75

Enter Pistol, Bardolph, and Page

PISTOL

God save you, Sir John.

FALSTAFF

Welcome, Ensign Pistol. Here, Pistol, I charge you with a cup
of sack. Do discharge yourself upon mine hostess.

PISTOL

I will discharge upon her, Sir John, with two bullets.

FALSTAFF

She is Pistol-proof. Sir; you shall hardly harm her.   80

HOSTESS

Come, I'll drink no proofs nor no bullets. I'll drink no more than will do me good, for no man's pleasure, I.

PISTOL

Then to you, Mistress Dorothy! I will charge you.

DOLL TEARSHEET

Charge me? I reject you, scurvy companion. What, you poor, base, rascally, cheating, shirtless mate! Away, you mouldy 85 rogue, away! I am meat for your master.

PISTOL

I know you, Mistress Dorothy.

DOLL TEARSHEET

Get, you cutpurse rascal, you filthy bung, away! By this wine, I'll thrust my knife in your mouldy chaps if you play the saucy bully with me. Away, you bottle-ale rascal, you postur- 90 ing passé poseur, you. Since when are you a soldier, I ask you, sir? Honest to god, all dressed for armour on your shoulder? As if!

PISTOL

God let me get my hands on you for this.

FALSTAFF

No more, Pistol. I would not have you go off here. Discharge 95 yourself away from our company, Pistol.

HOSTESS

No, good Captain Pistol, not here, sweet captain!

DOLL TEARSHEET

Captain? You abominable damned cheater, are you not ashamed to be called captain? If captains were of my mind, they would beat you for calling yourself a captain before you 100 have earned the name. You a captain? You slave, for what? For threatening a poor whore's neck in a bawdy-house? He a captain! Hang him, rogue.

41

BARDOLPH

I beg you calm down, good ensign.

FALSTAFF

Listen here, Mistress Doll. 105

PISTOL

Not I. I tell you what, Corporal Bardolph, I could split her. I'll
be revenged on her.

PAGE

Please, calm down.

PISTOL

I'll see her damned first; to Pluto's damned lake, by this hand,
to the infernal deep with Erebus and vile tortures. Hold 110
steady, I say. Have we not whoring here?

HOSTESS

Good Captain Pizzle, be quiet. It's very late, truly. I beseek
you now, aggravate your choler.

BARDOLPH

Be gone, good ensign. This will grow to a brawl shortly.

PISTOL

Let men die like dogs! Give crowns like pins! Do we not have 115
whoring here?

HOSTESS

On my word, captain, there's no such woman here. What the
hell, do you think I would deny her? For God's sake, be quiet.

PISTOL

Then feed, and be fat, my fair faint friend. Come, give us
some sack. 'Si fortune me tormente, sperato me contento.' 120
Afraid of attack? No, let the devil fire away. Give me some
sack, and, sweetheart, you lie there.

(laying down his sword)

Is that a full stop, then? And are etceteras nothing?

FALSTAFF

Pistol, I would be quiet.

PISTOL

Sweet knight, I kiss your fist. Come, we have seen   125
the seven stars together.

DOLL TEARSHEET

For God's sake, thrust him down stairs. I cannot endure such
a worthless rascal.

PISTOL

Thrust him down stairs? This from a common whore?

FALSTAFF

Pitch him down, Bardolph, like a game-piece shilling. No, if 130
he does nothing but speak nothing, he shall be nothing here.

BARDOLPH

Come, you get down stairs.

PISTOL

What! Shall we have incision? Shall we shed blood?

(snatching up his sword)

Then death rock me asleep, cut short my dismal days. Why,
then, let grievous, ghastly, gaping wounds Untwine the Sis- 135
ters Three. Come, Atropos, I say!

HOSTESS

This ought to be good!

FALSTAFF

Give me my rapier, boy.

DOLL TEARSHEET

I beg you, Jack, I beg you, do not draw.

FALSTAFF

You get down stairs.   140

Drawing, and driving Pistol out

HOSTESS

Here's a great tumult. I'll give up running this tavern, before

43

I'll put up with these terrors and frights. So, murder, I gather now. Enough, enough, put away your naked weapons, put away your naked weapons.

Exeunt Pistol and Bardolph

DOLL TEARSHEET

I beg you, Jack, be quiet. The rascal's gone. Ah, you wretched 145 little valiant villain, you!

HOSTESS

You're not hurt in the groin? I thought he made a sharp thrust at your belly.

Re-enter Bardolph

FALSTAFF

Have you tossed him out of doors?

BARDOLPH

Yes, sir. The rascal's drunk. You have hurt him, sir, in the 150 shoulder.

FALSTAFF

A rascal to challenge me!

DOLL TEARSHEET

Ah, you sweet little rogue, you. Oh my, poor ape, how you sweat! Come, let me wipe your face. Come on, you wretched chubby cheeks. Ah, rogue, I swear, I love you. You are as val- 155 orous as Hector of Troy, worth five of Agamemnon, and ten times better than the Nine Worthies. Ah, villain!

FALSTAFF

A rascally slave! I will toss the rogue in a laundry basket.

DOLL TEARSHEET

Do, if you dare for your heart. If you do, I'll toss you between a pair of sheets. 160

FALSTAFF

Sit on my knee, Doll. A rascal bragging slave! The rogue fled from me like quicksilver.

DOLL TEARSHEET

Truly, and you followed him like a church. You wretched little plump barbecue boar-pig, when will you leave fighting by day and thrusting by night and begin to patch up your old 165 body for heaven?

Enter, behind, Prince Henry and Poins, disguised

FALSTAFF

Hush, good Doll. Do not speak like a death's-head; do not bid me consider my end.

DOLL TEARSHEET

Mister, what is the prince's disposition like?

FALSTAFF

A good shallow young fellow, he would have made a good 170 scullery-maid; he would have trimmed bread well.

DOLL TEARSHEET

They say Poins has a good wit.

FALSTAFF

He a good wit? Hang him, baboon. His wit's as thick as mustard. A hammer has more imagination.

DOLL TEARSHEET

Why does the Prince love him so then?   175

FALSTAFF

Because their legs are both the same size, and he plays at tossing horseshoes well, and stomachs greasy food and sauce, and drinks flaming brandies, and plays riding the wild-mare with the boys, and breeds no strife with telling of discreet stories, that show a weak mind and an able body, which is why the 180 Prince keeps him around; for the Prince himself is just the same. There is not a hair of a difference between them.

PRINCE HENRY

Should this wretched round man have his ears cut off?

POINS

Let's beat him before his whore.

FALSTAFF

Kiss me, Doll. 185

PRINCE HENRY

Saturn and Venus this year in conjunction! What does the almanac have to say to that?

FALSTAFF

You give me the most flattering kisses.

DOLL TEARSHEET

I swear, these kisses come from the bottom of my heart.

FALSTAFF

I am old, I am old. 190

DOLL TEARSHEET

I love you better than I could ever love any scurvy young boy.

FALSTAFF

What material will you have a gown made of? I shall receive money on Thursday: you will have a cap tomorrow. A merry song! Come: it grows late. We'll to bed. You'll forget me when I am gone. 195

DOLL TEARSHEET

I swear, you'll start me weeping if you talk so. See if I ever dress myself beautifully until your return. Well, wait and see.

FALSTAFF

Some sack, Francis.

PRINCE HENRY, POINS

Right away, sir.

Coming forward

FALSTAFF

Ha? A bastard son of the King's? — And are you not Poins' 200 brother?

PRINCE HENRY

Why, you globe of sinful continents, what kind of a life do you lead?

FALSTAFF

A better one than you. I am a gentleman. You are a tapster.

PRINCE HENRY

Very true, sir, and I come to tap you about the ears.   205

HOSTESS

Oh, the Lord preserve your good Grace! Truly, welcome to London. Now, the Lord bless that sweet face of yours. Oh, Jesus, have you come from Wales?

FALSTAFF

You wretched mad mass of majesty, by this weak flesh and corrupt blood, you are welcome.   210

DOLL TEARSHEET

What? You fat fool! To hell with you.

POINS

My lord, he will turn this all into a joke and thwart your revenge if you do not strike while the iron is hot.

PRINCE HENRY

You wretched endless tub of tallow, you, how vilely did you speak of me even now before this honest, virtuous, civil gen-   215
tlewoman!

HOSTESS

God bless your good heart, and so she is, I swear.

FALSTAFF

Did you hear me?

PRINCE HENRY

Yes, and you knew me, as you did when you ran away by Gad's Hill. You knew I was at your back, and spoke it on pur-   220
pose to try my patience.

FALSTAFF

No, no, no, not so. I did not think you were within hearing.

PRINCE HENRY

I shall drive you then to confess the wilful abuse, and then I will know how to handle you.

FALSTAFF

No abuse, Hal, on my honor, no abuse.   225

PRINCE HENRY

Not to disparage me, and call me scullery-maid and bread-trimmer and I know not what?

FALSTAFF

No abuse, Hal.

POINS

No abuse?

FALSTAFF

No abuse, Ned, in the world, honest Ned, none. I maligned   230
him before the wicked, so that the wicked would not fall in love with you; in so doing, I have played the part of a careful friend and a true subject, and your father should give me thanks for it. No abuse, Hal. None, Ned, none. No, I swear, boys, none.   235

PRINCE HENRY

Is she of the wicked, is your hostess here of the wicked, or honest Bardolph, whose zeal burns in his nose, of the wicked?

POINS

Answer, you deadwood, answer.

FALSTAFF

The devil has marked Bardolph as irrecoverable, and his face is Lucifer's kitchen, where he does nothing but roast drunk-   240
ards.

PRINCE HENRY

For the women?

FALSTAFF

One of them, she is in hell already and burns poor souls. As
for the other, I owe her money, and if she is damned for that,
is not for me to say.   245

Knocking within

HOSTESS

Who knocks at the door so loud? Get the door there, Francis.

Enter Peto

PRINCE HENRY

Peto, what's up, what news?

PETO

The King your father is at Westminster,
And there are twenty weary messengers
Come from the north, and, as I came along   250
I met and overtook a dozen captains,
Bareheaded, sweating, knocking at the taverns
And asking every one for Sir John Falstaff.

PRINCE HENRY

By heaven, Poins, I now feel some remorse
For wasting precious time so idly   255
When storm of insurrection, like the south
Full of black vapour, does begin to melt
And drop upon our bare unarmoured heads. —
Give me my sword and cloak. — Falstaff, good night.

Prince, Poins, Peto exit

FALSTAFF

Now comes in the sweetest morsel of the night, and we must 260
go and leave it unpicked.

Knocking within. Bardolph exits.

More knocking at the door!

Re-enter Bardolph

What now, what's the matter?

BARDOLPH

You must depart for court, sir, instantly.

A dozen captains at the door for you.   265

FALSTAFF *(to the Page)*

Pay the musicians, boy. — Farewell, hostess. — Farewell, Doll. You see, my good wenches, how men of merit are sought after. The good-for-nothing may sleep when the man of action is called on. Farewell, good wenches. If I am not sent away immediately, I will see you again before I go.   270

DOLL TEARSHEET

I cannot speak. My heart is ready to burst — well, sweet Jack, take care of yourself.

FALSTAFF

Farewell, farewell.

Exeunt Falstaff and Bardolph

HOSTESS

Well, farewell. I will have known you twenty-nine years, come harvest-time, but an honester and truer-hearted man   275 — well, farewell.

BARDOLPH *(within)*

Mistress Tearsheet!

HOSTESS

What's the matter?

BARDOLPH *(within)*

Bid Mistress Tearsheet come to my master.

HOSTESS

Oh, run, Doll, run, run, good Doll.   280

They exit

ACT 3 ◆ SCENE 1

WESTMINSTER, THE PALACE

Enter King Henry IV in his nightgown, with a Page

KING HENRY IV

Go call the Earls of Surrey and of Warwick;
Before they come, bid them review these letters
Considering their contents well. Make speed.

Exit Page

How many thousand of my poorest subjects
Are at this hour asleep! Oh sleep, oh gentle sleep,   5
Nature's soft nurse, how have I frightened you,
That you no more will weigh my eyelids down
And steep my senses in forgetfulness?
Why would you rather lie in smoky cribs,
Upon uneasy pallets stretching you,   10
And hushed with buzzing night-flies to your slumber,
Than in the perfumed chambers of the great,
Under the canopies of costly state,
And lulled with sound of sweetest melody?
Oh drowsy god, why lie you with the vile   15
In loathsome beds, and leave the kingly couch
To keep the watch or toll the alarm bell?
Will you upon the high and giddy mast
Seal up the ship-boy's eyes and rock his brains
In cradle of the rude imperious surge   20
And in the visitation of the winds,
Who take the ruffian whitecaps by the top,
Curling their monstrous heads and hanging them
With deafening noise in the slippery clouds
That such a clamour death itself awakes?   25

Can you, oh partial sleep, give your repose
To the wet sea-boy in an hour so rude,
And, in the calmest and most stillest night,
Deny it to a king? Then, happy low, lie down.
Uneasy lies the head that wears a crown. 30

Enter Warwick and Surrey and Sir John Blunt

WARWICK

Many good mornings to your majesty.

KING HENRY IV

Is it the morning, lords?

WARWICK

It's one o'clock, and past.

KING HENRY IV

Why, then, good morning to you all, my lords.
Have you reviewed the letter that I sent you? 35

WARWICK

We have, my lord.

KING HENRY IV

Then you can see the body of our kingdom
How foul it is, what rank diseases grow,
And with what danger, near the heart of it.

WARWICK

It is like a body fighting illness, 40
Which to his former strength may be restored
With good advice and little medicine.
Northumberland's hot head will soon be cooled.

KING HENRY IV

Oh God, that one might read the book of fate
And see the revolution of the times 45
Make mountains level, and the continent,
Weary of solid firmness, melt itself
Into the sea. Oh, if all this were seen,

52

The happiest youth, viewing his progress through,
What perils past, what crosses yet to bear,   50
Would shut the book, sit himself down and die.
It has not been ten years
Since Richard and Northumberland, great friends,
Did feast together, and within two years
They were at wars. And only eight years since   55
Northumberland was nearest to my soul,
Who like a brother toiled in my affairs
And laid his love and life under my foot,
Who would take my part, defying Richard,
Even to his face. But which of you was by —   60
You, cousin Nevil, as I do remember —

(to Warwick)

When Richard, with his eye brimming with tears,
Rebuked and chastised by Northumberland,
Did speak these words, now proved a prophecy?
'Northumberland, you are the step by which   65
My cousin Bolingbroke ascends my throne' —
Though then, God knows, I had no such intent,
But when the state was in such dire need
I was compelled to accept greatness' kiss —
'The time will come,' he did go on to say,   70
'The time will come that foul sin, gathering head,
Shall break into corruption' — so went on,
Foretelling this very condition
And the division of our fellowship.

WARWICK

There is a history in all men's lives,   75
Examining the nature of times gone by,
That once observed, a man may prophesy,
With some accuracy, how certain things

May come to pass, their chance that in their seeds
And weak beginnings lie awaiting life.   80
Such things become the hatch and brood of time,
And by such inevitability,
King Richard might hazard a perfect guess
That great Northumberland, then false to him,
Would from that seed grow to a greater falseness,   85
Which should not find a ground to root upon
Unless on you.

KING HENRY IV

Are these things inevitable?
Then let us meet them as inevitable.
And that same word even now cries out on us.   90
They say the bishop and Northumberland
Are fifty thousand strong.

WARWICK

It cannot be, my lord.
Rumour does double, like the voice and echo,
The numbers of the feared. I urge your Grace   95
To go to bed. Upon my soul, my lord,
The powers that you already have sent forth
Will return victors very easily.
To comfort you some more, I have received
A confirmation that Glendower is dead.   100
Your Majesty has been these two weeks ill,
And these erratic hours can only add
Ill to your sickness.

KING HENRY IV

I will take your counsel.
And once internal wars are well in hand,   105
We will, dear lords, make for the Holy Land.

Exeunt

ACT 3 ◆ SCENE 2

GLOUCESTERSHIRE, BEFORE SHALLOW'S HOUSE

Enter Shallow and Silence, meeting; Mouldy, Shadow, Wart,
Feeble, Bullcalf, a Servant or two with them

SHALLOW

Come on, come on, come on. Give me your hand, sir, give me
your hand, sir. And how does my good cousin Silence?

SILENCE

Good morrow, good cousin Shallow.

SHALLOW

And how is my young cousin William? He is still at Oxford,
is he not?   5

SILENCE

Indeed, sir, at my cost.

SHALLOW

He'll be called to the Inns o' Court shortly. I was once of
Clement's Inn, where I think they will talk of mad Shallow
yet.

SILENCE

You were called 'lusty Shallow' then, cousin.   10

SHALLOW

By God, I was called any thing, and I would have done any
thing indeed too, and roundly too. There was I, and little John
Doit of Staffordshire, and black George Barnes, and Francis
Pickbone, and Will Squeal, a Cotswold man. You never saw
such four swashbucklers in all the Inns o' Court again. And   15
I may say to you, we knew where the good wenches were
and had the best of them all at our command. Then was Jack
Falstaff, now Sir John, a boy, and page to Thomas Mowbray,
Duke of Norfolk.

SILENCE

This Sir John, cousin, who comes here shortly about soldiers? 20

55

SHALLOW

The same Sir John, the very same. I saw him break Scoggin's head at the court gate, when he was a lad just this high; and the very same day did I fight with one Sampson Stockfish, a fruiterer, behind Grey's Inn. Lord, Lord, the mad days that I have spent! And to see how many of my old acquaintances 25 are dead.

SILENCE

We shall all follow, cousin.

SHALLOW

Certain, it's certain, very sure, very sure. Death, as the Psalmist said, is certain to all. All shall die. How much is a good yoke of bullocks at Stamford fair? 30

SILENCE

In truth, cousin, I was not there.

SHALLOW

Death is certain. Is old Dooble of your town living yet?

SILENCE

Dead, sir.

SHALLOW

Lord, Lord, dead! He drew a good bow, and dead? He shot a fine shot. He would have hit the bullseye at two hundred 35 forty yards, that it would have done a man's heart good to see. How much is twenty ewes now?

SILENCE

Depending on the quality, twenty good ewes may be worth ten pounds.

SHALLOW

And is old Dooble dead? 40

SILENCE

Here come two of Sir John Falstaff's men, I think.

Enter Bardolph and one with him

SHALLOW

Good morning, honest gentlemen.

BARDOLPH

Excuse me, which is Justice Shallow?

SHALLOW

I am Robert Shallow, sir, a poor esquire of this county, and
one of the King's justices of the peace. What is it that you   45
want with me?

BARDOLPH

My captain, sir, commends him to you, my captain, Sir John
Falstaff, a valiant gentleman, by heaven, and a most gallant
leader.

SHALLOW

He greets me well, sir.   50

Enter Falstaff

Look, here comes good Sir John. — Give me your good
hand, give me your Worship's good hand. I swear, you haven't
changed a bit. Welcome, good Sir John.

FALSTAFF

I am glad to see you well, good Master Robert Shallow. —
And Master Safe-bet, I think?   55

SHALLOW

No, Sir John. It is my cousin Silence, in commission with me.

FALSTAFF

Good Master Silence, it is appropriate you should be of the
peace.

SILENCE

Your good Worship is welcome.

FALSTAFF

Damn, this is hot weather, gentlemen. Have you provided me   60
here half a dozen capable men?

SHALLOW

Indeed, have we, sir. Will you sit?

FALSTAFF

Let me see them, please.

SHALLOW

Where's the roll? Where's the roll? Where's the roll? Let me
see, let me see, let me see. So, so, so, so, so. So, so. Yes, well 65
then, sir. — Rafe Mouldy! — Let them appear as I call, let
them do so, let them do so. Let me see, where is Mouldy?

MOULDY

Here, sir.

SHALLOW

What do you think, Sir John? A good-limbed fellow, young,
strong, and of good friends. 70

FALSTAFF

Is your name Mouldy?

MOULDY

Yes, sir.

FALSTAFF

It's more than time you were used.

SHALLOW

Ha, ha, ha, most excellent, by god! Things that are mouldy
lack use. Good one, in truth. Well said, Sir John, very well 75
said.

FALSTAFF

Prick him down.

MOULDY

I was pricked down well enough before, if you could have let
me alone. My old woman will be undone now with no one
to do her husbandry and her drudgery. You need not to have 80
chosen me. There are other men fitter than me to go out.

FALSTAFF

Go on. Peace, Mouldy. You will go. Mouldy, it is time you were spent.

MOULDY

Spent!

SHALLOW

Peace, fellow, peace. Stand aside. Do you know where you 85
are? — For the next, Sir John. Let me see. — Simon Shadow!

FALSTAFF

Yes, indeed, let me have him to sit under. He's like to be a cool soldier.

SHALLOW

Where's Shadow?

SHADOW

Here, sir. 90

FALSTAFF

Shadow, whose son are you?

SHADOW

My mother's son, sir.

FALSTAFF

Your mother's son! Sure enough, and your father's shadow.

SHALLOW

Do you like him, Sir John?

FALSTAFF

Shadow will serve for the summer. Prick him down, for we 95
have a number of shadows to fill up the muster-book.

SHALLOW

Thomas Wart!

FALSTAFF

Where's he?

WART

Here, sir.

FALSTAFF

Is your name Wart? 100

WART

Yes, sir.

FALSTAFF

You are a very ragged wart.

SHALLOW

Shall I prick him down, Sir John?

FALSTAFF

It's unnecessary. Prick him no more.

SHALLOW

Ha, ha, ha! You are funny, sir, you are funny. I'll give you that. 105
— Francis Feeble!

FEEBLE

Here, sir.

FALSTAFF

What trade are you, Feeble?

FEEBLE

A woman's tailor, sir.

SHALLOW

Shall I prick him, sir? 110

FALSTAFF

You may: but if he had been a man's tailor, he'd have pricked
you. — Will you make as many holes in an enemy's soldiers
as you have done in a woman's petticoat?

FEEBLE

I will do my best, sir. I can do no more.

FALSTAFF

Well said, good woman's tailor, well said, courageous Feeble! 115
You will be as valiant as the wrathful dove or most magnan-
imous mouse. — Prick the woman's tailor well, Master Shallow, deep, Master Shallow.

FEEBLE

I wish Wart might have gone, sir.

FALSTAFF

I wish you were a man's tailor, that you might mend him and 120
make him fit to go. Let that suffice, most forcible Feeble.

FEEBLE

It shall suffice, sir.

FALSTAFF

I am bound to you, reverend Feeble. — Who is next?

SHALLOW

Peter Bullcalf of the village green!

FALSTAFF

Yes, indeed, let's see Bullcalf. 125

BULLCALF

Here, sir.

FALSTAFF

By God, a likely fellow. Come, prick Bullcalf till he roars again.

BULLCALF

Oh Lord, good my lord captain —

FALSTAFF

What, do you roar before you are pricked?

BULLCALF

Oh Lord, sir, I am a diseased man. 130

FALSTAFF

What disease do you have?

BULLCALF

A wretched cold, sir, a cough, sir, which I caught ringing the
church bells upon the King's coronation day, sir.

FALSTAFF

Come, you shall go to the war in a dressing gown. — Is this all?

SHALLOW

That is two more than you asked for. You have four here, sir, 135 and so I pray you go in with me to dinner.

FALSTAFF

Come, I will go drink with you, but I cannot stay to dinner. I am glad to see you, by god, Master Shallow.

SHALLOW

Oh, Sir John, do you remember that time we lay all night in the windmill in Saint George's field? 140

FALSTAFF

No more of that, good Master Shallow, no more of that.

SHALLOW

Ha, that was a merry night. And is Jane Nightwork alive?

FALSTAFF

She lives, Master Shallow.

SHALLOW

She never could stand me.

FALSTAFF

Never, never. She always said she could not stand Master 145 Shallow.

SHALLOW

By god, I could anger her to the heart. She was then a good wench. Does she hold her own well?

FALSTAFF

Old, old, Master Shallow.

SHALLOW

Well, she must be old. She cannot help but be old. Certain 150 she's old, she had already had Robin Nightwork, old Night-work's son, before I came to Clement's Inn.

SILENCE

That's fifty-five year ago.

SHALLOW

Ha, cousin Silence, if you had seen what this knight and I have seen! — Ha, Sir John, am I right? 155

FALSTAFF

We have heard the chimes at midnight, Master Shallow.

SHALLOW

That we have, that we have, that we have. In truth, Sir John, we have. Our motto was 'Bottoms up, boys!' Come, let's go to dinner, come, let's go to dinner. Lord, the days that we have seen! Come, come.   160

Exeunt Falstaff and Justices

BULLCALF

Good Master Corporate Bardolph, be a friend, and here's four old ten shillings in French crowns for you. In very truth, sir, I would rather be hanged, sir, than go. And yet, for my own part, sir, I do not care; but rather, because I am unwilling, and, for my own part, have a desire to stay with my friends.   165 Otherwise, sir, I do not care, for my own part, so much.

BARDOLPH

Go on. Stand aside.

MOULDY

And, good Master Corporal Captain, for my old woman's sake, be a friend. She has nobody to do any thing for her when I am gone, and she is old and cannot help herself: I'll   170 give you forty, sir.

BARDOLPH

Fine then. Stand aside.

FEEBLE

By god, I do not care. A man can die but once. We owe God a death. I'll never stoop so low. If it is my destiny, so be it; if it is not, it's not. No man is too good to serve his prince, and   175 whichever way it goes, he that dies this year is paid for the next.

BARDOLPH

Well said. You are a good fellow.

FEEBLE

Truth, I'll never stoop so low.

Re-enter Falstaff and the Justices

FALSTAFF

Come, sir, which men shall I have?   180

SHALLOW

Whichever four you please.

BARDOLPH

Sir, a word with you. I have three pound to free Mouldy and
Bullcalf.

FALSTAFF

Good work.

SHALLOW

Come, Sir John, which four will you have?   185

FALSTAFF

You choose for me.

SHALLOW

Well, then, Mouldy, Bullcalf, Feeble and Shadow.

FALSTAFF

Mouldy and Bullcalf! For you, Mouldy, stay at home till you
are too old to serve. — And for your part, Bullcalf, grow until
you are old enough. I want none of you.   190

SHALLOW

Sir John, Sir John, do not make a mistake here. They are the
best men, and I would have you served with the best.

FALSTAFF

Will you tell me, Master Shallow, how to choose a man?
Do I care for the limb, the sinews, the stature, bulk and big
appearance of a man? Give me the spirit, Master Shallow.   195
Here's Wart. You see what a ragged appearance he has. He
shall load and discharge as steadily as a tinsmith's hammer.
And this same slender fellow, Shadow, give me this man. He

64

presents no mark to the enemy. The enemy may as well take
aim at the edge of a penknife. And for a retreat, how swiftly 200
will this Feeble, the woman's tailor, run off! Oh, give me the
spare men, and spare me the great ones. — Put a musket into
Wart's hand, Bardolph.

BARDOLPH

Here, Wart. Fall in. Attention. Present arms.

FALSTAFF

Come, manage your musket: so, very well, go on, very good, 205
exceedingly good. Oh, give me always a little, lean, old,
chapped, bald marksman. Well said, in truth, Wart. You are
a good scab.

SHALLOW

He has not mastered the craft. He does not do it right. I
remember at Mile End Green, when I lay at Clement's Inn 210
— I played King Arthur's fool in the show — there was a little nimble fellow, and he would handle his weapon like this.
And he would run about and run about, and come at you and
come at you. 'Rah, tah, tah,' he would say. 'Boom' he would
say, and away he would go again, and again he'd come. I have 215
never seen such a fellow.

FALSTAFF

These fellows will do fine, Master Shallow. — God bless you,
Master Silence. I will not use many words with you. Farewell, gentlemen. I thank you both. I must make a dozen miles
tonight. — Bardolph, give the soldiers coats. 220

SHALLOW

Sir John, God watch over your affairs. At your return visit our
house. Let our old acquaintance be renewed. Perhaps I will
go with you to the court.

FALSTAFF

By God, I wish you would, Master Shallow.

SHALLOW

Go on. I mean what I say. God keep you. 225

FALSTAFF

Farewell, gentle gentlemen.

Exeunt Justices

On, Bardolph. Lead the men away.

Exeunt Bardolph, Recruits, & c

When I return, I will exploit these justices. I do see right
through Justice Shallow. Lord, Lord, how liable we old men
are to this vice of lying. This same starved justice has done 230
nothing but boast to me of the wildness of his youth and the
feats he has done about Turnbull Street, and every third word
a lie, paid quicker to the hearer than taxes to the crown. I do
remember him at Clement's Inn, looking like a man made
from a leftover cheese-rind. When he was naked, he was, for 235
all the world, like a forked radish, with a head fantastically
carved upon it with a knife. He was so skeletal that his dimen-
sions to anyone with poor eyesight were invisible. He was
the very embodiment of famine, yet lecherous as a monkey,
and the whores called him 'mandrake.' And now this Vice's 240
dagger has become a squire, and now he has fertile land and
fat oxen. Well, I'll renew our acquaintance if I return, and it
will take some work but I will make him a steady stream of
wealth for me. If the little fish is bait for the big fish, I see no
reason in the law of nature that I cannot snap at him. But 245
time will tell, and that is that.

Exit

ACT 4 ◆ SCENE 1

YORKSHIRE, GAULTREE FOREST

Enter the Archbishop of York, Mowbray, Lord Hastings,
Colevile, and others

ARCHBISHOP OF YORK

What is this forest called?

HASTINGS

It's Gaultree Forest, if it please your Grace.

ARCHBISHOP OF YORK

Stand here, my lords, and send our scouts ahead

To learn the numbers of our enemies.

HASTINGS

We've sent them forth already.   5

ARCHBISHOP OF YORK

It's well done.

My friends and brethren in these great affairs,

I must inform you that I have received

Most recent letters from Northumberland,

The dire and chilling contents of them this: 10

He does retreat to Scotland, there to raise

An army, and concludes in hearty prayers

That your attempts in battle may prevail

Against the mighty powers of the foe.

MOWBRAY

And so the hopes we had in him touch ground   15

And dash themselves to pieces.

Enter a Messenger

HASTINGS

Now, what news?

67

MESSENGER

> West of this forest, scarcely off a mile,
> The enemy comes on in massive strength,
> And, from the ground they cover, I estimate   20
> They number thirty thousand men or more.

MOWBRAY

> The very number that we thought they had.
> Let us march on and face them in the field.

ARCHBISHOP OF YORK

> What well-appointed leader meets us here?

Enter Westmoreland

MOWBRAY

> I think it is my Lord of Westmoreland.   25

WESTMORELAND

> Health and fair greeting from our general,
> The Prince, Lord John and Duke of Lancaster.

ARCHBISHOP OF YORK

> Do tell, my Lord of Westmoreland, in peace,
> The purpose of your coming.

WESTMORELAND

> Then, my lord,   30
> The substance of my speech I do address
> Primarily to your Grace. You, Lord Archbishop,
> Who does project both peace and innocence,
> How can it be that you translate yourself
> Out of the speech of peace, that bears such grace,   35
> Into the harsh and savage tongue of war.

ARCHBISHOP OF YORK

> How can I do this? We are all diseased
> And with our greedy self-indulgent lives
> Have worked ourselves into a burning fever,
> And we must bleed for it. Hear me more plainly.   40

I have in equal balance justly weighed
What wrongs our arms may do, what wrongs we suffer,
And find our griefs heavier than our offences.
We see which way the stream of time does run
And we are forced from our most quiet lives   45
By the rough torrent of circumstance.
When we are wronged and would outline our griefs,
We are denied access unto the king
By the very men who have most done us wrong.
The dangers of the days just barely past,   50
Whose memory is written on the earth
With still apparent blood, and the examples
Of every minute's instance, present now,
Has put us in these unbecoming arms,
Not to break peace or any branch of it,   55
But to establish here authentic peace,
Concurring both in name and quality.

WESTMORELAND
When was it that your appeal was denied?
In what way were you injured by the king,
That you would seal this lawless bloody book   60
Of forged rebellion with a seal divine?

ARCHBISHOP OF YORK
For all my brothers, in the commonwealth,
I make my quarrel in particular.

WESTMORELAND
There is no need of any such redress,
Or if there were, it is not owed to you.   65

MOWBRAY
Why not to him in part, and to us all
That feel the bruises of the days before
And suffer the condition of these times?

WESTMORELAND

Oh, my good Lord Mowbray,

Acknowledge that the times do call the tune,   70

And you shall say it is the circumstance,

And not the King, that does you injuries.

Yet for your part, it does not seem to me

Either from the King or in the circumstance

That you should have an inch of any ground   75

To build a grief on. Was the entire estate

Of your noble, well remembered father,

The Duke of Norfolk, not returned to you?

MOWBRAY

What thing, in honor, had my father lost

That need to be revived and breathed in me?   80

King Richard loved him, but was as things stood,

Against his will compelled to banish him.

WESTMORELAND

You don't know what you speak of, Lord Mowbray.

If your father had been victor there,

He never would have escaped the city;   85

For all the country in united voice

Cried hate upon him; and all their prayers and love

Were set on Bolingbroke, who they adored

And blessed and graced, more than Richard the King.

But this is mere digression from my purpose.   90

I come here from our princely general

To know your griefs, to tell you from his Grace

That he will give you audience; wherever

It shall appear that your demands are just,

They shall be met.   95

MOWBRAY

But he has forced us to compel this offer,

And it proceeds from craftiness, not love.
WESTMORELAND
Mowbray, you show contempt to take it so.
This offer comes from mercy, not from fear.
For, look, within your view our army lies,   100
Distinguished soldiers populate our ranks,
Our men more perfect in the use of arms,
Our armour all as strong, our cause the best.
It stands to reason that our heart's as good.
Do not suggest our offer is coerced.   105
MOWBRAY
Well, by my will we shall attend no parley.
WESTMORELAND
That only proves the shame of your offence.
A rotten case withstands no handling.
HASTINGS
Does Prince John have a full commission,
The authorization of his father,   110
To hear and to address with independence
Just what conditions we insist upon?
WESTMORELAND
That is implicit in the General's name.
I wonder that you even question it.
ARCHBISHOP OF YORK
Then take this document, Lord Westmoreland, this schedule,   115
For this contains our general grievances.
If each separate article is addressed,
And if the scattered members of our cause
Are all acquitted by true legal means,
And our demands for redress are achieved   120
In reference to the wrongs done just to us,
We will fall in, and march in line again

And knit our powers to the arm of peace.
WESTMORELAND
This I will show the General. Please you, lords,
In sight of both our we may meet;   125
And either end in peace, God will it so!
Or to the field of battle call the swords
Which must decide it.
ARCHBISHOP OF YORK
My lord, we will do so.

Exit Westmoreland

MOWBRAY
My heart still whispers they will not agree   130
To any small conditions of our peace.
HASTINGS
Do not fear that. If we can make our peace
Upon such large terms and so absolute
As our conditions shall insist upon,
Our peace shall stand as firm as rocky mountains.   135
MOWBRAY
Yes, but our valuation shall be such
That every rumour and each perceived slight,
Shall taste of rebellion to the King.
ARCHBISHOP OF YORK
No, no, my lord. Note this: the King is weary
Of minor and such trifling grievances,   140
For he has found to end one doubt by death
Revives two greater in those who survive.
He cannot so precisely weed this land
As his suspicions would have him do;
His foes are so enrooted with his friends   145
That, plucking to evict an enemy,
He does unfasten so and shake a friend;

HASTINGS

    Besides, the King has wasted all his rods

    On fresh offenders, so he now does lack

    The very instruments of chastisement,   150

    So that his power, like of a fangless lion,

    May threaten but not hold.

ARCHBISHOP OF YORK

    It's very true,

    And therefore be assured, my good Lord Mowbray,

    If we do make our reconcilement well,   155

    Our peace will, like a broken limb united,

    Grow stronger for the breaking.

MOWBRAY

    I hope so.

    Look here, my Lord of Westmoreland returns.

                   Re-enter Westmoreland

WESTMORELAND

    The Prince is here at hand. Please it your Lordship   160

    To meet his Grace halfway between our armies.

MOWBRAY

    Your Grace of York, in God's name then, set forth.

ARCHBISHOP OF YORK

    Before, and greet his Grace. My lord, we come.

                   All move forward

LANCASTER

    You are well encountered here, my cousin Mowbray.

    Good day to you, gentle Lord Archbishop,   165

    And so to you, Lord Hastings, and to all.

    My Lord of York, it did become you more

    When your good flock, assembled by the bell,

    Encircled you to hear with reverence

    Your exposition on the holy text   170

Than now to see you here, a warrior talking,
Urging a rout of rebels with your drum,
Turning the word to sword, and life to death.
Oh, you misuse the reverence of your place,
Employ the trappings and the grace of heaven   175
To cover shameful deeds, as a false favourite
Uses his prince's name. You have enrolled,
The subjects of God's substitute, the King,
Under the counterfeited zeal of God,
And both against the peace of heaven and him   180
Have here inflamed them.

ARCHBISHOP OF YORK

My good Lord of Lancaster,
I am not here against your father's peace,
But, as I told my Lord of Westmoreland,
These stormy times and truly, common sense,   185
Force us to act in monstrous seeming ways
To keep our persons safe. I sent your Grace
The details and particulars of our grief,
Which scornfully rejected from the court,
Did cause this Hydra son of war be born,   190
Whose dangerous eyes may well be charmed asleep
If granted our most just and right desires,
And madness cured, show true obedience,
Stoop tamely to the foot of majesty.

MOWBRAY

If not, we are prepared to take our chances   195
To the last man.

HASTINGS

And if we should fail here,
We have supplies to second our attempt:
If they do flounder, theirs shall second them,

And so success of mischief shall be born,   200
And heir from heir shall carry on this fight
Each English generation to the next.

LANCASTER

You are too shallow, Hastings, much too shallow
To sound the bottom of eternity.

WESTMORELAND

Perhaps your Grace should answer them directly   205
And share your thoughts about their grievances.

LANCASTER

I do agree they are legitimate,
And swear here by the honor of my blood
My father's goals have been misunderstood,
And some around him overstepped their bounds   210
In executing acts in his behalf.
My lord, these griefs shall be redressed with speed;
I swear to it, they shall. If this does please you,
Discharge your powers back to their separate counties,
As we will ours, and here, between the armies,   215
Let's drink together friendly and embrace,
That all their eyes may bear those tokens home
Of our restored love and amity.

ARCHBISHOP OF YORK

I take your princely word you'll make amends.

LANCASTER

I give it you, and will maintain my word,   220
And on that word I drink health to your Grace.

HASTINGS

Go, captain, and deliver to the army
This news of peace. Let them have pay, and part.
I know it will please them well. Go now, captain.

Exit Officer

ARCHBISHOP OF YORK

    To you, my noble Lord of Westmoreland. 225

WESTMORELAND

    I pledge your Grace; and, if you knew the lengths

    That I have gone to breed this present peace,

    You would drink freely. But my love to you

    Shall show itself more openly from here.

ARCHBISHOP OF YORK

    I do not doubt you. 230

WESTMORELAND

    I am glad of it. —

    Health to my lord and gentle cousin, Mowbray.

MOWBRAY

    You wish me health at the opportune moment,

    For I am feeling suddenly quite ill.

ARCHBISHOP OF YORK

    Before disaster men are always merry, 235

    Foreboding does precede a good event.

WESTMORELAND

    Therefore be merry, cuz, since sudden sorrow

    Serves just to say: 'some good thing comes

    tomorrow.'

ARCHBISHOP OF YORK

    Believe me, I am very light in spirit. 240

MOWBRAY

    So much the worse if your own rule be true.

                Shouts within

LANCASTER

    The word of peace is rendered. Hear how they shout.

MOWBRAY

    It sounds like cheering after victory.

ARCHBISHOP OF YORK

A peace is very like a victory,

Both noble parties cease to bear their arms,   245

And neither party loses.

LANCASTER

Go, my lord,

And let our army also be discharged.

Exit Westmoreland

And, let us, my good lord, have all our troops

March by us, that we may peruse the men   250

We might have fought against.

ARCHBISHOP OF YORK

Go, good Lord Hastings,

And, before dismissing them, let them march by.

Exit Hastings

LANCASTER

I trust, lords, we shall stay together tonight.

Re-enter Westmoreland

Now, cousin, why does our army still stand?   255

WESTMORELAND

The leaders, having heard from you to stand,

Will not go off until they hear you speak.

LANCASTER

They follow orders.

Re-enter Hastings

HASTINGS

My lord, our army is dispersed already.

Like youthful steers unyoked, they've headed off   260

East, west, north, south, or, as released from school,

Each hurries toward his home and sporting-place.

WESTMORELAND

Good tidings, my Lord Hastings, since that's done,

I do arrest you, traitor, for high treason. —
And you, Lord Archbishop, and you, Lord Mowbray,   265
For capital treason I arrest you both.

MOWBRAY

Is this proceeding just and honourable?

WESTMORELAND

Was your rebellion so?

ARCHBISHOP OF YORK

You'll break your faith with us?

LANCASTER

I pledged you none.   270
I promised you redress of these same grievances
Of which you did complain, which, by my honor,
I will perform with a most Christian care.
But rebels, you will, get what you deserve
For the rebellion and these acts of yours.   275
Most foolishly you raised these arms,
Unwisely brought them here and then sent hence. —
Strike up our drums; pursue the scattered stray.
God, and not we, has safely fought today. —
Some guard these traitors to the block of death,   280
Treason's true bed and yielder-up of breath.

Exeunt

ACT 4 ♦ SCENE 2

ANOTHER PART OF THE FOREST

Alarum. Excursions.

Enter Falstaff and Colevile, meeting

FALSTAFF

What's your name, sir? Of what position are you, and of what place, I pray?

COLEVILE

I am a knight, sir, and my name is Colevile of the Dale.
Are you not Sir John Falstaff?

FALSTAFF

As good a man as he, sir, whoever I am. Do you yield, sir, or   5
shall I sweat for you? If I do sweat, they are the teardrops of
your lovers, and they weep for your death. Therefore rouse
up fear and trembling, and do observance to my mercy.

COLEVILE

I think you are Sir John Falstaff, and in that case, surrender
myself.   10

FALSTAFF

I have a whole school of tongues in this belly of mine, and
every tongue speaks nothing but my name. If I had an ordi-
nary belly, I'd be nothing more than the most active fellow
in Europe. My gut, my gut, my gut undoes me. Here comes
our general.   15

Enter Prince John of Lancaster, Westmoreland, Blunt, and others

LANCASTER

The danger's past. Follow no further now.
Call in the armies, good cousin Westmoreland.

Exit Westmoreland

Now, Falstaff, where have you been all this while?
When everything is ended, then you come.
These tardy tricks of yours will, on my life,   20
Some day find you climbing the gallows' steps.

FALSTAFF

I am sorry, my lord, that you think it so. I never knew that
rebuke and reproach was the reward of valour. Do you think I
am a swallow, an arrow, or a bullet? Can I in my poor and old
motion travel at the speed of thought? I have speeded here   25
as quickly as possible. I have worn out a hundred and eighty

plus horses, and here, travel-tainted as I am, have in my pure and immaculate valour, taken Sir John Colevile of the Dale, a most furious knight and valorous enemy. But what of that? He saw me and yielded, that I may justly say, with the noble- 30 nosed fellow of Rome, 'I came, saw, and overcame.'

LANCASTER

It was more of his courtesy than your deserving.

FALSTAFF

I don't know about that. Here he is, and here I surrender him. And I beseech your Grace, let it be documented with the rest of this day's deeds, or, I swear, I will have it immortalised in a 35 ballad, with my own picture on the top of it, Colevile kissing my foot; which if I am forced to do, if you do not all look as dull as counterfeit coins beside me, and I in the clear sky of fame overshine you as much as the full moon does the stars, mere pins' heads compared to her, do not believe the word 40 of the noble. Therefore let me have my due, and let the accumulation mount.

LANCASTER

Yours is too heavy to mount.

FALSTAFF

Let it shine, then.

LANCASTER

Yours is too thick to shine. 45

FALSTAFF

Let it do something, my good lord, that may do me good, and call it what you will.

LANCASTER

Is your name Colevile?

COLEVILE

It is, my lord.

LANCASTER

You are a famous rebel, Colevile. 50

FALSTAFF

And a famous true subject took him.

COLEVILE

I am, my lord, just as my betters are

That led me here. Had they been ruled by me,

Your victory would have cost you so much more.

FALSTAFF

I know not how they sold themselves, but you, like a kind 55

fellow, gave yourself away gratis, and I thank you for that.

Re-enter Westmoreland

LANCASTER

Now, have you quit pursuit?

WESTMORELAND

Retreat is made and execution stayed.

LANCASTER

Send Colevile with his confederates

To York, to speedy execution. — 60

Soldier, lead him from here, and guard him well.

Exeunt Blunt and others with Colevile

Now let us proceed toward the court, my lords.

I hear the King my father has grown sick.

Our news shall go before us to his Majesty,

Which, cousin, you shall bear to comfort him, 65

And we with sober speed will follow you.

FALSTAFF

My lord, I beg you give me leave to go

Through Gloucestershire, and, when you come to court,

That I may stand, lord, in your good report.

LANCASTER

Fare you well, Falstaff. That I speak of you 70

At all shall speak better than you deserve.

Exeunt all but Falstaff

FALSTAFF

I wish you had the wit; it would serve you better than your
dukedom. Good god, this same young sober-blooded boy
does not love me, nor can a man make him laugh. But that's
not surprising; he drinks no wine. None of these demure   75
boys come to anything, for thin drink does so overcool their
blood, that they fall into a kind of swooning anemia, and
then, when they marry, they produce only girls. They are
generally fools and cowards, which some of us should be too,
but for inebriation. A good sherry sack has a two-fold oper-   80
ation in it. It ascends into the brain, and dries all the foolish
and dull and cruddy vapours that gather there, makes it per-
ceptive, quick, creative, full of nimble, fiery, and delectable
shapes, which, delivered over to the voice, the tongue, is born
as excellent wit. The second property of your excellent sherry   85
is the warming of the blood, which, left to itself, is cold and
sluggish and makes the liver white and pale, which is the
badge of faintheartedness and cowardice. But the sherry
warms it and makes it course from the internal organs to the
extremities. It illuminates the face, which as a beacon rouses   90
all the rest of this little kingdom that is man; and then the
vital commoners and inland petty spirits rally round to their
captain, the heart, who, great and puffed up with this retinue,
does any deed of courage, and this valour comes of sherry.
And this is how it is that Prince Harry is valiant, for the cold   95
blood he did naturally inherit from his father which is like
lean, sterile, and bare land, he has manured, husbanded, and
tilled with excellent endeavour of drinking good and good
store of fertile sherry, that he has become very hot and valiant. If I had a thousand sons, the first human principle I   100

would teach them should be to forswear thin libations and to
addict themselves to sack.

Enter Bardolph

How now, Bardolph?

BARDOLPH

The army is all discharged and gone.

FALSTAFF

Let them go. I'll go through Gloucestershire, and there will   105
I visit Master Robert Shallow, Esquire. I have him already
softening between my finger and thumb, and shortly we will
seal the deal. Come away.

Exeunt

ACT 4 ♦ SCENE 3

WESTMINSTER, THE JERUSALEM CHAMBER

*Enter King Henry IV, the Princes Thomas of Clarence
and Humphrey of Gloucester, Warwick, and others*

KING HENRY IV

Now, lords, if God does grant us victory
In this discord that's bleeding at our doors,
We will our youth lead on to higher fields
And draw swords only that are sanctified.
Our navy is prepared, our power collected,   5
Our deputies commissioned and empowered,
And every wish we have is within reach.
We only lack a little personal strength;
So wait until these rebels now afoot
Come underneath the yoke of government.   10

WARWICK

Both which we do not doubt your Majesty
Shall soon enjoy.

KING HENRY IV
Humphrey, my son of Gloucester, where is the
Prince your brother?

GLOUCESTER
I think he's gone to hunt, my lord, at Windsor.   15

KING HENRY IV
And how accompanied?

GLOUCESTER
I do not know, my lord.

KING HENRY IV
Is not his brother Thomas of Clarence with him?

GLOUCESTER
No, my good lord, he is attendant here.

CLARENCE
Your wish, my lord and father?   20

KING HENRY IV
Nothing but well to you, Thomas of Clarence.
How chance you are not with the Prince your brother?
He loves you, and you do neglect him, Thomas.
You have a better place in his affection
Than all your brothers. Cherish it, my boy,   25
And you may find that you can mediate
Between his greatness and your other brothers,
When I am dead. Therefore neglect him not,
Be mindful that you do not blunt his love,
Nor lose the good advantage of his grace   30
By seeming cold or careless of his will.
For if respected, he can be most kind,
He has a tear for pity and a hand
Both generous and strong with charity;
Yet notwithstanding, being incensed he is flint.   35
His temper, therefore, must be well observed.

Chide him for faults, and most respectfully,
When you perceive his blood inclined to mirth;
Learn this, Thomas,
And you shall prove a shelter to your friends,   40
A hoop of gold to bind your brothers in.

CLARENCE

I shall observe him with all care and love.

KING HENRY IV

Why are you not at Windsor with him, Thomas?

CLARENCE

He is not there today; he dines in London.

KING HENRY IV

And how accompanied? Can you tell that?   45

CLARENCE

With Poins and his customary followers.

KING HENRY IV

Most subject is the richest soil to weeds,
And he, the noble image of my youth,
Is overspread with them; therefore my grief
Stretches itself beyond the hour of death.   50
The blood weeps from my heart when I allow
Myself to imagine the lawless days
And rotten times that you shall look upon
When I am sleeping with my ancestors.
For when his headstrong riot has no curb,   55
When rage and hot blood are his counsellors,
When he has both the means and inclination,
Oh, with what wings shall his affections fly
Directly into danger and decay!

WARWICK

My gracious lord, you misinterpret him.   60
The Prince just studies his companions

Like a strange tongue, in that to learn the language,
It's crucial that the most immodest word
Be looked upon and learned; which, once attained,
Your Highness knows, comes to no further use   65
But to be known and hated. So, like gross terms,
The Prince will, when the time is opportune,
Cast off his followers, and their memory
Shall as a guideline or a lesson live,
By which his grace measures the lives of others,   70
Turning past evils to advantages.

KING HENRY IV

The bee will rarely leave the home she's built,
In carrion or not.

Enter Westmoreland

Who's here? Westmoreland?

WESTMORELAND

Health to my sovereign, and new happiness   75
Added to that that I am to deliver.
Your son Prince John does kiss your Grace's hand.
Mowbray, the Bishop Scroop, Hastings and all
Are brought to the correction of your law.
There is now not a rebel's sword unsheathed   80
But peace puts forth her olive everywhere.

KING HENRY IV

Oh Westmoreland, you are a summer bird,
Which in the dying days of winter sings
The breaking of the day.

Enter Harcourt

Look, here's more news.   85

HARCOURT

Heaven keep your Majesty from enemies,
And when they stand against you, may they fall

As those that I have come to tell you of.
The Earl Northumberland and the Lord Bardolph,
With a great power of English and of Scots,   90
Are taken by the sheriff of Yorkshire.
This packet, if you please, contains in full
The manner and true order of the fight.

KING HENRY IV

And why should all this good news make me sick?
Will Fortune never come with both hands full?   95
She either gives a stomach and no food —
Or else a feast and takes away the stomach.
I should rejoice now at this happy news,
And yet my sight fails, and my brain is giddy.
Oh come near me, now, I am very ill.   100

GLOUCESTER

Comfort, your Majesty!

CLARENCE

Oh, my royal father!

WESTMORELAND

My sovereign lord, bear up yourself, courage.

WARWICK

Be patient, princes. You do know these fits
Come on his Highness very frequently.   105
Stand from him, give him air. He'll be well soon.

CLARENCE

No, no, he cannot long withstand these pangs.

GLOUCESTER

I fear the signs, for people do report
The birth of babies unholy and deformed.
The seasons change their course, as if the year   110
Had found some months asleep and overleaped them.

CLARENCE

    The river flooded three times without cease,

    And the elders who remember these things

    Say this is how it happened just before

    Our great-grandfather, Edward, suddenly died.   115

WARWICK

    Speak lower, princes, for the King recovers.

GLOUCESTER

    This apoplexy will surely be his end.

KING HENRY IV

    I pray you take me up and bear me hence

    Into some other chamber. Softly, pray.

        The King is carried to a bed on another part of the stage.

KING HENRY IV

    Set me the crown upon my pillow here.   120

CLARENCE

    His eyes are sunken, and he changes much.

                Enter Prince Henry

PRINCE HENRY

    Who's seen the Duke of Clarence?

CLARENCE

    I am here, brother, full of heaviness.

PRINCE HENRY

    What's this, then, rain indoors, and none outside?

    How is the King?   125

GLOUCESTER

    Extremely ill.

PRINCE HENRY

    Has he heard the good news yet? Tell him.

GLOUCESTER

    He was affected upon hearing it.

PRINCE HENRY

If he is sick with joy, he'll recover without medicine.

WARWICK

Not so much noise, my lords. — Sweet prince, speak low.   130
The King your father is trying to sleep.

CLARENCE

Let us withdraw into the other room.

WARWICK

Will it please your Grace to go along with us?

PRINCE HENRY

No, I will sit and watch here by the King.

Exeunt all but Prince Henry

Why does the crown lie there upon his pillow,   135
Being so troublesome a bedfellow?
Oh polished perturbation, golden care,
That keeps the ports of slumber open wide
To many a watchful night! Sleep with it now;
Yet not so sound nor half so deeply sweet   140
As he whose brow with homely nightcap bound
Snores out the watch of night. Oh majesty,
When you do pinch your bearer, you do sit
Like a rich armour worn in heat of day,
That scalds with safety. By his gates of breath   145
There lies a downy feather which lies still;
If he did breathe, that light and weightless down
Would have to stir. My gracious lord, my father,
This sleep is sound indeed. This is a sleep
That from this golden circle has divorced   150
So many English kings. My due to you
Is tears and heavy sorrows of the blood,
Which nature, love, and filial tenderness
Shall, O dear father, pay you generously.

Your due to me is this imperial crown, 155
Which, as your first born son and rightful heir
Is handed down to me. Here, here it sits,
Which God shall guard. This heavy crown from you
Will I leave to mine, as you left to me.

Exit

KING HENRY IV

Warwick! Gloucester! Clarence! 160

Re-enter Warwick, Gloucester, Clarence, and the rest

CLARENCE

Does the King call?

WARWICK

What do you need, your Majesty? Your Grace?

KING HENRY IV

Why did you leave me here alone, my lords?

CLARENCE

We left the Prince my brother here, my lord,
Who took it on himself to sit by you. 165

KING HENRY IV

The Prince of Wales! Where is he? Let me see him:
He is not here.

WARWICK

This door is open. He is gone this way.

GLOUCESTER

He did not come through the room where we stayed.

KING HENRY IV

Where is the crown? Who took it from my pillow? 170

WARWICK

When we withdrew, my lord, we left it here.

KING HENRY IV

The prince has taken it. Go, seek him out.
Is he so hasty that he does suppose my sleep my death?

Find him, my Lord of Warwick. Bring him here.

Exit Warwick

The way he acts conjoins with my disease   175
And helps to end me. See, sons, what things you are,
How quickly nature falls into revolt
When gold becomes her object!
For this the foolish overcareful fathers
Disturb their sleep with thoughts,   180
Their brains with care, their bones with industry.
For this they have collected and piled up
The tarnished heaps of questionable gold;
For this they have most thoughtfully brought up
Their sons with arts and martial exercises —   185

Re-enter Warwick

Now, where is he who will not stay so long
Till his friend sickness puts an end to me?

WARWICK

My lord, I found the Prince in the next room,
His gentle cheeks awash with kindly tears.

KING HENRY IV

But why then did he take away the crown?   190

Re-enter Prince Henry

Here, here he comes. — Come here to me, Harry. —
Depart the chamber. Leave us here alone.

Exeunt Warwick and the rest

PRINCE HENRY

I never thought to hear you speak again.

KING HENRY IV

You wished that, Harry, and you thought it so.
I live too long for you; I weary you.   195
Do you so hunger for my empty chair
That you do need to seize upon my crown

Before your time is come? Oh foolish youth,
You seek the greatness that will overwhelm you.
You have stolen that which would in hours   200
Be yours without offence, and at my death
You have confirmed my expectation.
Your life did show me that you loved me not,
And you will have me die assured of it.
You hide a thousand daggers in your thoughts,   205
Which you have whetted on your stony heart
To stab at half an hour of my life.
What, can you not indulge me half an hour?
Then get you gone and dig my grave yourself,
And bid the merry bells ring to your ear   210
That you are crowned, and not that I am dead.
Give that which gave you life back to the worms.
Pluck down my officers, break my decrees,
For now the time is come to mock at form.
Harry the Fifth is crowned. Up, vanity,   215
Down, royal state, all you sage counsellors, go.
And to the English court assemble now,
From every region, apes of idleness.
Now, all you sewers, purge you of your scum.
Have you a ruffian that will swear, drink, dance, 220
Revel the night, rob, murder, and commit
The oldest sins in newest kind of ways?
Be happy, he will trouble you no more.
England shall double gild his treble guilt,
England shall give him office, honor, might,   225
For the fifth Harry from curbed licence plucks
The muzzle of restraint, and the wild dog
Shall flesh his tooth on every innocent.
Oh my poor kingdom, sick with civil blows!

When my good care could not withhold your riots,   230
What will you do when riot is your care?
Oh, you will be a wilderness again,
Peopled with wolves, your old inhabitants.

PRINCE HENRY

Oh pardon me, my lord! Only my tears,
Kept me from stopping this most harsh rebuke   235
Before you spoke in grief and I had heard
This much of it so far. There is your crown,
May He that wears the crown immortally
Long guard it yours. If I regard it more
Than as your honor and as your renown,   240
Let me no more from this obedience rise,
As this prostrate and exterior bending
Reflects my inward true and duteous spirit.
As God is my witness, when I came in,
And found no course of breath within your Majesty,   245
My heart froze in my chest! If I do feign,
Oh, let me in my present wildness die
And never live to show the doubting world
The noble change I have been planning.
Coming to look on you, thinking you dead,   250
And dead almost, my lord, to think you were,
I spoke as if this crown could hear my voice,
And so upbraided it: 'The care on you depending
Has fed upon the body of my father;
Therefore you best of gold are worst of gold.   255
Other, less fine in carat, is more precious,
But you, most fine, most honoured: most renowned,
Devoured up your bearer.' Thus, my most royal lord,
Accusing it, I put it on my head
To duel with it, as with an enemy   260

Who had before my eyes murdered my father.
But if it did infect my blood with joy,
Or swell my thoughts to any strain of pride,
If any rebel or vain spirit of mine
Did with the least affection of a welcome   265
Give entertainment to the might of it,
Let God forever keep it from my head
And make me as the poorest subject is
That does with awe and terror kneel to it.

KING HENRY IV   270
Oh my son,
God put it in your mind to take it then,
That you might win more of your father's love,
Pleading so wisely in excuse of it.
Come here, my Harry, sit you by my bed
And hear, I think, the very final counsel   275
That I shall ever breathe. God knows, my son,
By what circuitous and crooked ways
I took this crown, and I myself know well
How troublesome it sat upon my head.
To you it shall descend with better quiet,   280
Better opinion, better confirmation,
For all the soil of the achievement goes
With me into the earth. It seemed on me
An honor snatched with violent savage hands,
And many living who reminded me   285
Of their assistance in the gain of it,
Which daily grew to quarrel and to bloodshed,
Wounding the cause of peace. All these bold fears
You see with peril I have answered,
For all my reign has been an effort to   290
Address that argument. And now my death

Changes the mood, for what in me was purchased
Falls upon you in a more fairer sort.
So you assume the crown successively.
Yet though you stand more sure than I could do,   295
You are not strong enough, since griefs are green,
And all my friends, which you must make your friends,
Have been disarmed, but only recently.
Since through their efforts I was first advanced,
I feared that they would use their powers to   300
Displace me once again; which to avoid,
I cut them off; and had a purpose now
To lead out many to the Holy Land,
Since rest and lying still might make them look
Too closely at my state. Therefore, my Harry,   305
Make it your plan to busy giddy minds
With foreign quarrels, that action, so borne out,
Erase the memory of the former days.
More would I, but my lungs are wasted so
That strength of speech is utterly denied me.   310
How I came by the crown, O God forgive;
And grant it may with you in true peace live.

PRINCE HENRY

My gracious lord,
You won it, wore it, kept it, gave it me.
Then plain and right must my possession be,   315
Which I with more than with a common pain
'Gainst all the world will rightfully maintain.

Enter Lord John of Lancaster

KING HENRY IV

Look, look, here comes my John of Lancaster.

LANCASTER

Health, peace, and happiness to my royal father.

KING HENRY IV

You bring me happiness and peace, son John,   320
But health, I fear, with youthful wings has flown
From this bare withered trunk. Upon your sight
My worldly business makes a period.
Where is my Lord of Warwick?

PRINCE HENRY

My Lord of Warwick.   325

Enter Warwick, and others

KING HENRY IV

Does any name particular belong
To that first chamber where I did collapse?

WARWICK

It's called Jerusalem, my noble lord.

KING HENRY IV

Praise be to God! And there my life must end.
It has been prophesied to me many years,   330
I should not die but in Jerusalem;
Which vainly I supposed the Holy Land.
But bear me to that chamber; there I'll lie.
In that Jerusalem shall Henry die.

Exeunt

ACT 5 ◆ SCENE 1

GLOUCESTERSHIRE, SHALLOW'S HOUSE

Enter Shallow, Falstaff, Bardolph, and Page

SHALLOW

By cake and capon, sir, you shall not leave tonight. — Oh,
Davy, I say!

FALSTAFF

You must excuse me, Master Robert Shallow.

SHALLOW

I will not excuse you. You shall not be excused. Excuses shall
not be admitted. There is no excuse shall serve. You shall not   5
be excused. — Oh, Davy!

Enter Davy

DAVY

Here, sir.

SHALLOW

Davy, Davy, Davy, Davy, let me see, Davy, let me see, Davy,
let me see. Yes, indeed, William the cook, tell him come here.
— Sir John, you shall not be excused.   10

SHALLOW

Some pigeons, Davy, a couple of short-legged hens, a joint
of mutton, and any pretty little tasty dishes, tell William to
cook.

DAVY

Does the soldier stay all night, sir?

SHALLOW

Yes, Davy, I will host him well. A friend in the court is better   15
than a penny in the purse. Treat his men well, Davy; for they
are degenerate rogues and will backbite.

DAVY

No worse than they are back-bitten, sir, for they have wretch-
edly foul linen.

SHALLOW

Good one, Davy. About your business, Davy.   20

DAVY

I urge you, sir, to look favourably on William Visor of Won-
cot against Clement Perkes of the hill.

SHALLOW

There are many complaints, Davy, against that Visor. That
Visor is a rogue, to my knowledge.

DAVY

I grant your worship that he is a rogue, sir, but   25
yet, God forbid, sir, that a rogue should be denied favour at
his friend's request. The rogue is my honest friend, sir; therefore, I urge you look upon him favourably.

SHALLOW

Go on, I say, he will not be wronged. Now, mind, Davy.

Exit Davy

Where are you, Sir John? Come, come, come, off with your 30
boots. — Give me your hand, Master Bardolph.

BARDOLPH

I am glad to see your Worship.

SHALLOW

I thank you with all my heart, kind
Master Bardolph, and welcome, my tall fellow.

(to the Page)

— Come, Sir John.   35

FALSTAFF

I'll follow you, good Master Robert Shallow.

Exit Shallow

Bardolph, look to our horses.

Exeunt Bardolph and Page

It is a wonderful thing to see the similarity of his men's spirits and his. They, by observing him, do bear themselves like foolish justices; he, by consorting with them, is turned into a justice-like servingman. If I wanted something from Master Shallow, I would cultivate his men by appearing to be close to their master: if from his men, I would flatter Master Shallow that no man could better command his servants. It is certain that either wise bearing or ignorant comportment is caught, as men catch diseases from one another. Therefore men should take heed of their company. I will gather enough material out of this Shallow to keep Prince Harry in continual laughter for a year.

SHALLOW *(within)*

Sir John!

FALSTAFF

I come, Master Shallow, I come, Master Shallow.

Exit

ACT 5 ◆ SCENE 2

WESTMINSTER, THE PALACE

Enter Warwick and the Lord Chief Justice, meeting

WARWICK

Here, my Lord Chief Justice, where you off to?

CHIEF JUSTICE

How is the king?

WARWICK

He's very well. His cares are now all ended.

CHIEF JUSTICE

I hope, not dead.

WARWICK

He's walked the way of nature,

And to our purposes he lives no more.

CHIEF JUSTICE

I wish his Majesty had called me with him.
The loyalty with which I served his life
Has left me vulnerable with his death.

WARWICK

Indeed I think the young king loves you not.   10

CHIEF JUSTICE

I know he does not, and do arm myself
To bear whatever hardship comes of this,
The truth of which can hardly be as bad
As my imagination conjures it.

Enter Lancaster, Clarence, Gloucester, Westmoreland, and others

WARWICK

Here come the grieving sons of dead Harry.   15
Oh that the living Harry had the temper
Of he who is the least of these brothers!
Then noble men might safely hold their places,
And not be pushed aside by commoners!

CHIEF JUSTICE

Oh God, I fear all will be overturned.   20

LANCASTER

Good morning, cousin Warwick, good morning.

GLOUCESTER, CLARENCE

Good morning, cousin.

LANCASTER

We meet like men forgotten how to speak.

CHIEF JUSTICE

Peace be with us, lest we be heavier.

GLOUCESTER

Oh, my good lord, you have lost a friend indeed.   25

LANCASTER

    Though no man can be sure what grace he'll find,

    You can of all of us expect the least.

    I am sorry and wish it wasn't so.

CLARENCE

    You must now speak well of Sir John Falstaff,

    Which goes against your nature and your place.   30

CHIEF JUSTICE

    Sweet princes, what I did, I did in honor,

    Led by the impartial conduct of my soul;

    And you will never see me begging for

    A forced and inauthentic pardon.

    If truth and upright innocence fail me,   35

    I'll to the king my master who is dead

    And tell him who has sent me after him.

WARWICK

    Here comes the Prince.

                Enter King Henry V, attended

CHIEF JUSTICE

    Good morning, and God save your Majesty!

KING HENRY V

    This new and gorgeous garment majesty   40

    Sits not so easy on me as you think.

    Brothers, you mix your sadness with some fear.

    This is the English, not the savage court,

    Where brother cuts his rival brothers down,

    To safeguard his seat. Yet be sad, good brothers,   45

    For, by my faith, it very well becomes you.

    Sorrow so royally in you appears

    That I will gravely put the fashion on

    And wear it in my heart. Why then, be sad.

    But you do not bear it alone, good brothers,   50

It's a joint burden laid upon us all.
For me, by heaven, I bid you be assured,
I'll be your father and your brother too.
Let me but bear your love, I'll bear your cares.
Yet weep that Harry's dead; and so will I,   55
But Harry lives, who will convert those tears
One by one into hours of happiness.

PRINCES

We hope no other from your Majesty.

KING HENRY V

You all look strangely on me. And you most.
You are, I think, convinced I love you not.   60

CHIEF JUSTICE

I am convinced, if my acts are judged fairly,
Your Majesty has no just cause to hate me.

KING HENRY V

No? How might a prince of my great hopes forget
The great indignities you laid upon me?
Berate, rebuke, and roughly send to prison   65
The immediate heir of England? Was this easy?
This memory washed away, and forgotten?

CHIEF JUSTICE

I then did represent the king your father,
As his sovereign power was vested in me.
And, in the administration of his law,   70
While I was working for the commonwealth,
Your highness purposely ignored my place,
And struck me in my very seat of judgement,
And since your actions an offence against
Your father, I used my authority   75
And did commit you. If the deed was wrong,
Would you be contented, now you are king,

To have a son flout your decrees outright?
To scorn the judges you have set in place?
To warp the course of law and blunt the sword   80
That guards the peace and safety of your person?
And worse, to disregard your royal image
And mock your directions in your deputy?
Question your royal thoughts, make the case yours;
Be now the father and think of a son,   85
See your most solemn laws so rashly slighted,
Behold yourself so by a son disdained,
And then imagine me taking your part
And in your name gently silencing your son.
After this consideration, sentence me,   90
And, as you are a king, explain to me
What I have done that was above my place,
My person, or my lord's sovereignty.

KING HENRY V
You are right, justice, and you judge this well.
Therefore still wear the office and the sword.   95
And I do wish your honors may increase,
Till you do live to see a son of mine
Offend you and obey you as I did.
You did commit me into the hands of justice
For which I do commit into your hand   100
The unstained sword that you have borne so far,
With this reminder: that you use its weight
With the same bold, just, and impartial spirit
As you did against me. There is my hand.
You shall be as a father to my youth.   105
My voice shall sound as you do prompt my ear,
And I will stoop and humble my intents
To your well-practised wise directions. —

And, princes all, believe me, I beseech you:
My father is gone wild into his grave,   110
For in his tomb now lie my wanton ways,
And with his sombre spirit I survive
To mock the expectation of the world,
To frustrate prophecies and to raze out
Rotten opinion, who has dismissed me   115
As so wanton. The tide of blood in me
Has proudly flowed in vanity till now.
Now it does turn and ebb back to the sea,
Where it shall mingle with the state of floods
And flow from now in formal majesty.   120
Now call we our high court of parliament,
And let us choose such limbs of noble counsel
That the great body of our state may go
In equal rank with the best governed nation;
That war, or peace, or both at once, may be   125
As things acquainted and familiar to us,
In which you, father, shall have foremost hand.
Our coronation done, we will call for,
As I before have mentioned, all our state.
And, God endorsing all my good intents,   130
No prince nor peer shall have just cause to say
God shorten Harry's happy life one day.

Exeunt

ACT 5 ◆ SCENE 3

GLOUCESTERSHIRE, SHALLOW'S ORCHARD

Enter Falstaff, Shallow, Silence, Davy, Bardolph, and the Page

SHALLOW

No, you shall see my orchard, where, in an arbor, we will eat
last year's apples of my own cultivation, with a dish of sweet-

meats, and so forth. Come, cousin Silence. — And then to
bed.

FALSTAFF

By God, you have a rich and ample dwelling here.   5

SHALLOW

Barren, barren, barren, beggars all, beggars all, Sir John.
Truly, good air. — Spread the table, Davy, spread the table,
Davy. Well done, Davy.

FALSTAFF

This Davy certainly does a lot for you. He is both servingman
and husband.   10

SHALLOW

A good servant, a good servant, a very good servant, Sir
John. By god, I have drunk too much sack at supper. A good
servant. Now sit down, now sit down. — Come, cousin.

SILENCE *(singing)*

Do nothing but eat, and make good cheer,
And praise God for the merry year,   15
When flesh is cheap and females dear,
And lusty lads roam there and here
So merrily,
And all the while so merrily.

FALSTAFF

There's a merry heart! — Good Master Silence, I'll drink your   20
health for that right away.

SHALLOW

Give Master Bardolph some wine, Davy.

DAVY

Sweet sir, sit. I'll be with you right away. Most sweet sir, sit.
Mister page, good mister page, sit.

SHALLOW

Be merry, Master Bardolph. — And, my little soldier there,   25

105

be merry.

SILENCE *(singing)*

Be merry, be merry, my wife has all,

For women are shrews, both short and tall.

'Tis merry in hall when beards wag all,

And welcome merry Shrovetide.   30

Be merry, be merry.

FALSTAFF

I did not think Master Silence to be a man of this mettle.

SILENCE

Who, I? I have been merry once or twice before now.

DAVY *(to Bardolph)*

— A cup of wine, sir.

SILENCE *(singing)*

A cup of wine that's brisk and fine,   35

And drink to you, oh mistress mine,

And a merry heart lives long-a.

FALSTAFF

Well said, Master Silence.

SILENCE

And we shall be merry; now comes in the best time of the

night.   40

FALSTAFF

Health and long life to you, Master Silence.

SILENCE *(singing)*

Fill the cup, and pass it round,

I'll drink to you right to the bottom.

SHALLOW

Honest Bardolph, welcome. — Welcome, my little tiny thief,

(to the Page) and welcome indeed too. I'll drink to Master   45

Bardolph, and to all the gallants about London.

DAVY

I hope to see London once before I die.

SHALLOW

By god, you'll crack a quart together, ha, will you not,
Master Bardolph?

BARDOLPH

And I'll stick by him, sir.   50

SHALLOW

Why, there spoke a king. Lack nothing, be merry.
(knocking within)

Look who's at door there. Who knocks?

Exit Davy

FALSTAFF

Why, now you have done me right.

To Silence, seeing him take off a bumper

SILENCE *(singing)*

Do me right,

And dub me knight   55

Fernando.

Is it not so?

FALSTAFF

It is so.

SILENCE

Is it so?

Re-enter Davy

DAVY

If it please your Worship, there's one Pistol come from the   60
court with news.

FALSTAFF

From the court? Let him come in.

Enter Pistol

How now, Pistol?

107

PISTOL

Sir John, God save you.

FALSTAFF

What wind blew you this way, Pistol?   65

PISTOL

Not the ill wind which blows no man to good. Sweet knight,
you are now one of the greatest men in this realm.

SILENCE

By god, I think he might be, except for Mister Puff of
Barson.

PISTOL

Puff?   70

Puff in your teeth, most cowardly trator base!—

Sir John, I am your Pistol and your friend,

And helter-skelter have I rode to you,

And tidings do I bring, and lucky joys,

And golden times, and happy precious news.   75

FALSTAFF

I urge you now, deliver them like a man of this world.

PISTOL

A curse upon the world and worldlings base!

I speak of Africa and golden joys.

FALSTAFF

Oh base Assyrian knight, what is your news?

Let your bounteous king know the truth of it.   80

SHALLOW

Beg your pardon, sir. If, sir, you come with news from the
court, I take it there's but two ways, either to utter them, or
to conceal them. I am, sir, under the King in some authority.

PISTOL

Under which king, beggar? Speak, or die.

SHALLOW

Under King Harry.   85

PISTOL

Harry the Fourth? or Fifth?

SHALLOW

Harry the Fourth.

PISTOL

A curse for your office! —

Sir John, your tender lambkin is now king.

Harry the Fifth's the man. I speak the truth.   90

FALSTAFF

What, is the old king dead?

PISTOL

As a doornail. The things I speak are true.

FALSTAFF

Away, Bardolph! — Saddle my horse. — Master Robert Shallow, choose what office you'd like in the land, it's yours. —
Pistol, I will over-load you with dignities.   95

BARDOLPH

Oh joyful day!

I would not take a knighthood for my fortune.

PISTOL

There, I do bring good news!

FALSTAFF

Carry Master Silence to bed. — Master Shallow, my Lord
Shallow, be what you will. I am Fortune's steward. Get on 100
your boots. We'll ride all night. — Oh sweet Pistol! — Away,
Bardolph!

Exit Bardolph

Come, Pistol, tell me more, and furthermore devise something to do yourself good. Boots, boots, Master Shallow. I
know the young king is sick for me. Let us take any man's 105

horses. The laws of England are at my commandment. Blessed are they that have been my friends, and woe to my Lord Chief Justice!

PISTOL

And let vile vultures seize upon his lungs!
'Where is the life I used to lead?' they say.   110
Why, here it is. Welcome these pleasant days.

Exeunt

ACT 5 ◆ SCENE 4

LONDON, A STREET

Enter Beadles, dragging in Hostess Quickly and Doll Tearsheet

MISTRESS QUICKLY

No, you wretched rogue. I would to God that I might die, so I might have you hanged. You have yanked my shoulder right out of the joint.

FIRST BEADLE

The constables have delivered her to me, and she shall have a public flogging soon enough, I promise. There's been a man   5
or two killed lately, and she's involved.

DOLL TEARSHEET

Nut-hook, nut-hook, you lie! Come on, I'll tell you what, you damn tripe-faced rascal: if the child I now am with does miscarry, you'd been better off striking your mother, you paperfaced villain.   10

MISTRESS QUICKLY

Oh the Lord, that Sir John would come! He would make somebody bleed for this. But I pray to God she does not miscarry the fruit of her womb.

FIRST BEADLE

If she does, you will have a dozen cushions again; you have only eleven now. Come, I charge you both to go with me, for   15 the man that you and Pistol beat amongst you is dead.

DOLL TEARSHEET

I'll tell you what, you insubstantial thin man, I will have you
soundly thrashed for this, you bluebottle rogue, you filthy
famished correctioner. If you are not thrashed, I'll give up
wearing skirts.   20

FIRST BEADLE

Come, come, you reprobate, come.

MISTRESS QUICKLY

Oh God, that right should ever overcome might! Well, of suf-
fering comes character.

DOLL TEARSHEET

Come, you rogue, come, bring me to a justice.

MISTRESS QUICKLY

Ay, come, you starved bloodhound.   25

DOLL TEARSHEET

Mister Reaper, Mister Bones!

MISTRESS QUICKLY

You skeleton, you!

DOLL TEARSHEET

Come, you thin thing, come, you rascal.

FIRST BEADLE

Very well.

Exeunt

ACT 5 ♦ SCENE 5

A PUBLIC PLACE NEAR WESTMINSTER ABBEY

Enter two Grooms, strewing rushes

FIRST GROOM

More rushes, more rushes.

SECOND GROOM

The trumpets have sounded twice.

FIRST GROOM

It will be two o'clock when they come from the
coronation. Hurry, hurry.

Exeunt

Enter Falstaff, Shallow, Pistol, Bardolph, and Page

FALSTAFF

Stand here by me, Master Robert Shallow. I will make the 5
King honor you. I will give him a look as he comes by, and
you observe the look that he will give me.

PISTOL

God bless your lungs, good knight!

FALSTAFF

Come here, Pistol, stand behind me. — Oh, if I had had time
to have made new clothing, I would have spent the thousand 10
pounds I borrowed from you. But no matter. This poor show
does better. This does imply the zeal I had to see him.

SHALLOW

So it does.

FALSTAFF

It shows my earnestness of affection —

SHALLOW

So it does. 15

FALSTAFF

My devotion —

SHALLOW

It does, it does, it does.

FALSTAFF

As it were, to ride day and night, and not to deliberate, not
to remember, not to have patience to change my clothes —

SHALLOW

It is best, for sure. 20

FALSTAFF

But to stand stained with travel, and sweating with desire to see him, thinking of nothing else, putting all affairs else in oblivion, as if there were nothing else to be done but to see him.

Shouts within, and the trumpets sound

PISTOL

There roared the sea, and trumpet-clangor sounds.   25

*Enter King Henry V and his train,
the Lord Chief Justice among them*

FALSTAFF

God save your grace, King Hal, my royal Hal!

PISTOL

The heavens guard and keep you, most royal imp of fame!

FALSTAFF

God save you, my sweet boy!

KING HENRY V

My Lord Chief Justice, speak to that vain man.

CHIEF JUSTICE

Have you your wits? Know you to whom you speak?   30

FALSTAFF

My king, my Jove! I speak to you, my heart!

KING HENRY V

I know you not, old man. Fall to your prayers.
How ill white hairs become a fool and jester!
I have long dreamed of such a kind of man,
So bloated and so old and so profane;   35
But now awake, I do despise my dream.
Reduce your body now, increase your grace;
Leave gormandizing. Know the grave does gape
Three times more wide for you than other men.
Do not reply to me with foolish jest.   40

Do not presume I am the thing I was.
For God does know — so shall the world perceive —
That I have now cast off my former self.
So will I those that kept me company.
When you do hear I am as I have been,   45
Approach me, and you shall be as you were,
The tutor and the feeder of my riots.
Till then I banish you, on pain of death,
As I have done the rest who did mislead me,
Not to come near our person by ten mile.   50
Enough to sustain life I will allow you,
That lack of means not drive you towards evil.
And, as we hear you do reform yourselves,
We will, according to your strengths and qualities,
Give you advancement. Be it your charge, my lord,   55
To see my order here is carried out. —
Onward.

Exeunt King Henry V, & c

FALSTAFF

Master Shallow, I owe you a thousand pound.

SHALLOW

Yes, indeed, Sir John, which I beseech you to let me
take home with me.   60

FALSTAFF

That can hardly be, Master Shallow. Do not grieve at this. I
shall be sent for in private to him. You see, he must seem this
way to the world. Do not fear for your prospects. I will yet be
the man who shall make you great.

SHALLOW

I don't know how that could be, unless you give me your dou-   65
blet and stuff me out with straw. I beg you, good Sir John, let
me have five hundred of my thousand.

FALSTAFF

Sir, I will be as good as my word. This that you heard was just a shadow.

SHALLOW

A shadow that I fear you will die in, Sir John. 70

FALSTAFF

Fear no shadows. Go with me to dinner. — Come, Lieutenant Pistol. — Come, Bardolph. — I shall be sent for soon at night.

Re-enter Prince John of Lancaster, the Lord Chief Justice;
Officers with them

CHIEF JUSTICE

Go, carry Sir John Falstaff to the jail.

Take all his company along with him.

FALSTAFF

My lord, my lord — 75

CHIEF JUSTICE

I cannot speak now. I will hear you soon. —

Take them away.

PISTOL

Si fortune me tormenta, spero me contenta.

Exeunt all but Prince John and the Lord Chief Justice

LANCASTER

I like this fair proceeding of the King's.

He does intend his former followers 80

Shall all be very well provided for,

But all are banished till their bad behaviors

Appear more wise and modest to the world.

CHIEF JUSTICE

And so they are.

LANCASTER

The King has called his parliament, my lord. 85

CHIEF JUSTICE

He has.

LANCASTER

I will lay odds, before this year expires,
We bear our civil swords and native fire
As far as France. I heard a bird sing so,
Whose music, to my thinking, pleased the King.   90
Come, will you go?

Exeunt

EPILOGUE

Spoken by a Dancer

If you look for a good speech now, then I am lost, for what I
have to say is of my own making, and what indeed I should
say will, no doubt, prove my own unmaking. But if you are
not too much clogged with fat meat, our humble author will
continue the story, with Sir John in it, and make you merry   5
with fair Katharine of France, where, for all I know, Falstaff
will die of a pox, unless he is already killed by your hard
opinions; for Oldcastle died a martyr, and this is not the man.
My tongue is weary; so I will bid you good night.